www.gowildnyc.org

# GO WILD
# in New York City

## BRAD MATSEN

### illustrations by PAUL CORIO

### scientific illustration by Kate Lake

**NATIONAL GEOGRAPHIC**

Washington, D.C.

# yo.

New York City can be pretty wild. But not the way you're thinking. I'm Skippy, an Eastern Gray Squirrel, and I'm a native New Yorker. I'll be accompanying you on your reading safari through the true wildness in New York City. By the time you're finished you'll know almost as much about going wild in New York as I do—give or take a few thousand years.

This book is dedicated to Ted Kheel.

Book design by Dillon Thompson LLC
The body text of the book is set in Bell Gothic. The display text is set in Slack Casual.

*Go Wild in New York City* is an Eye Candy Books, LLC, production.

Cataloging-in-Publication Data is available from the Library of Congress upon request.
ISBN: 0-7922-7982-4

Nurture New York's Nature is a not-for-profit foundation established to create public awareness of the importance of nurturing New York's nature for the health and well being of all its inhabitants. NNYN was launched in 2002 by Theodore W. Kheel with proceeds from an exclusive world-wide, royalty-free license granted by the artists Christo and Jeanne-Claude for The Gates, Project for Central Park, and additional support from Deutsche Bank, the law firm of Paul, Hastings, Janofsky & Walker, Verizon, and the Center for Environmental Research and Conservation. The foundation sponsors research, books, lectures, conferences, publicity campaigns and events, and encourages alliances among groups and organizations dedicated to resolving the conflicts between nature and development that arise in the urban environment. For more information about NNYN and how you can help nurture nature in the city, visit nnyn.org.

One of the world's largest nonprofit scientific and educational organizations, the National Geographic Society was founded in 1888 "for the increase and diffusion of geographic knowledge." Fulfilling this mission, the Society educates and inspires millions every day through its magazines, books, television programs, videos, maps and atlases, research grants, the National Geographic Bee, teacher workshops, and innovative classroom materials. The Society is supported through membership dues, charitable gifts, and income from the sale of its educational products. This support is vital to National Geographic's mission to increase global understanding and promote conservation of our planet through exploration, research, and education.

For more information, please call 1-800-NGS LINE (647-5463) or write to the following address:
NATIONAL GEOGRAPHIC SOCIETY
1145 17th Street N.W.
Washington, D.C. 20036-4688 U.S.A.

Visit the Society's Web site at www.nationalgeographic.com.

Printed in the United States of America

8 Water City

18 NYC Rocks!

28 Take a Deep Breath

36 Hey, Nice Plants!

46 Rulers of New York

56 Fur, Fins, Fangs, & Feathers

66 Food In, Garbage Out

74 Resources

# WATER CITY

**24 lbs!**

**WATER, WATER EVERYWHERE.** It's in the clouds, puddles, rivers and lakes around New York. But the way we get water in our sinks, showers, tubs, and toilets began with kids who had to carry it. Imagine. Every day, that's one of your chores. Get a bucket. Walk to a well dug in the ground. Fill the bucket from the well. Carry it home. Every gallon of water weighs eight pounds.

$H_2O =$

**TWO ATOMS OF HYDROGEN + ONE ATOM OF OXYGEN = WATER**

**3 GALLONS**

Each bucket holds about three gallons. That's twenty-four pounds. Are your arms sore? Today, the eight million or so people in New York City use about a billion and a half gallons of water each day. That's 500 million buckets. But where does it come from? How does it get to you? Somebody or something has to carry it. Does that faucet handle or shower head look like a miracle to you yet? Read on.

**FROM CREEKS TO GIANT TUNNELS**
THE HISTORY OF WATER IN NEW YORK CITY

BEFORE 1667 WATER CAME FROM RAIN AND STREAMS LIKE MINETTA CREEK AND LAKES LIKE THE COLLECT POND

1667 FIRST PUBLIC WELL IN NEW YORK CITY AT BOWLING GREEN

# WONDERFUL WATER MYSTERY TOUR

In the time line on these pages, you'll find clues to the locations of the earliest creeks, wells, and reservoirs of New York City. Today, they look like the pictures on the right. Can you guess where these are?

**1. THEN Reservoir, 1776**
*NOW Broadway between Pearl and White Streets*

**2. THEN Minetta Creek**
*NOW Minetta Street*

**3. THEN First public well, 1667**
*NOW Bowling Green and Broadway*

**4. THEN Croton Reservoir, 1842**
*NOW Croton Reservoir, Westchester County*

**5. THEN Reservoir, water mains, 1800**
*NOW Chambers Street*

**6. THEN The Collect Pond, 1667**
*NOW Criminal Courts Building*

**7. THEN Croton Aqueduct**
*NOW High Bridge, Harlem River*

**8. THEN End of Giant Tunnel #1**
*NOW Third Ave. and Schermerhorn, Brooklyn*

1776 FIRST NYC RESERVOIR ON BROADWAY BETWEEN PEARL AND WHITE STREETS

1798 BAD WATER = DISEASES SUCH AS YELLOW FEVER AND CHOLERA

1800 RESERVOIR ON CHAMBERS STREET AND WOODEN WATER PIPES BUILT

1830 FIRE TANK AND WELL, BROADWAY AND 13TH STREET BUILT

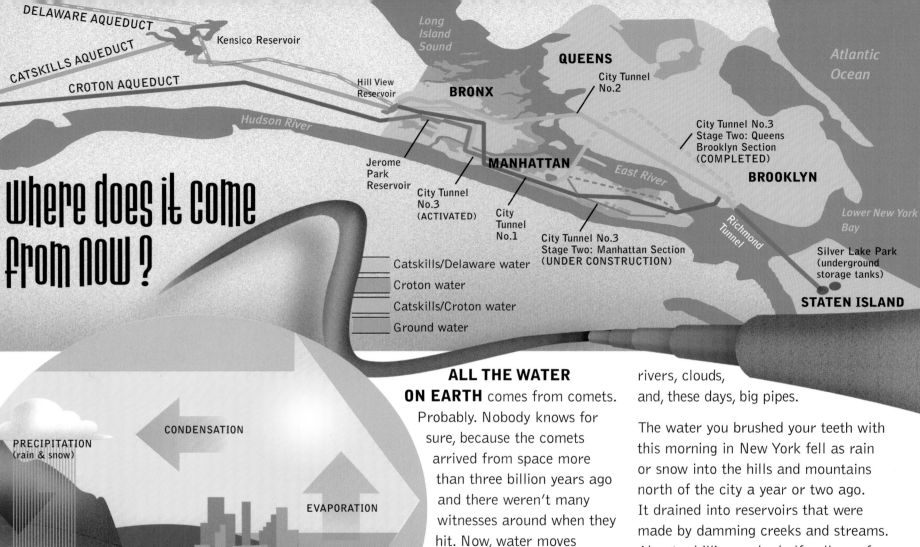

# Where does it come from now?

DELAWARE AQUEDUCT

CATSKILLS AQUEDUCT

CROTON AQUEDUCT

Kensico Reservoir

*Hudson River*

*Long Island Sound*

*Atlantic Ocean*

QUEENS

City Tunnel No.2

Hill View Reservoir

BRONX

City Tunnel No.3 Stage Two: Queens Brooklyn Section (COMPLETED)

Jerome Park Reservoir

MANHATTAN

*East River*

BROOKLYN

City Tunnel No.3 (ACTIVATED)

City Tunnel No.1

City Tunnel No.3 Stage Two: Manhattan Section (UNDER CONSTRUCTION)

*Richmond Tunnel*

*Lower New York Bay*

Silver Lake Park (underground storage tanks)

STATEN ISLAND

Catskills/Delaware water

Croton water

Catskills/Croton water

Ground water

## THE HYDROLOGIC CYCLE

CONDENSATION

PRECIPITATION (rain & snow)

EVAPORATION

UNDERGROUND LAKES AND STREAMS

AQUIFER

**ALL THE WATER ON EARTH** comes from comets. Probably. Nobody knows for sure, because the comets arrived from space more than three billion years ago and there weren't many witnesses around when they hit. Now, water moves around the planet in what is called the Hydrologic Cycle. Water changes to vapor and sometimes changes to snow or ice and then back to water again, moving from place to place in oceans, rivers, clouds, and, these days, big pipes.

The water you brushed your teeth with this morning in New York fell as rain or snow into the hills and mountains north of the city a year or two ago. It drained into reservoirs that were made by damming creeks and streams. About a billion and a half gallons of water from the reservoirs make their way into town every day through pipes and tunnels leading to two giant tunnels that run hundreds of feet deep under New York City.

1842 CROTON RIVER RESERVOIR AND AQUEDUCT FINISHED

1892 LAST NYC CHOLERA OUTBREAK

1915 ASHOKAN RESERVOIR AND CATSKILL SYSTEM FINISHED

1917 CITY WATER TUNNEL #1 COMPLETED

**PLAIN WATER? NO.**
Scientists test New York City water every day and sometimes add small amounts of chemicals to be sure the water is safe to drink and use for cooking.

FLUORIDE TO PREVENT TOOTH DECAY
SODIUM HYDROXIDE TO DECREASE THE ACID TASTE
CHLORINE TO KILL GERMS
ORTHOPHOSPHATE TO COAT PIPES TO KEEP LEAD OUT OF THE WATER

**BORING, BORING, BORING**
City Water Tunnel #3 is being built by a huge boring machine. The machine is 23 feet in diameter and weighs 450 tons. On its last job, it dug a railroad tunnel under the English Channel.

**City Water Tunnel #1**
was finished in 1917. It begins in Yonkers, ends up in Staten Island, and was drilled through solid rock 200 to 750 feet below ground level. Now, this same tunnel can carry a billion gallons of water every day. City Water Tunnel #2, finished in 1936, also begins in Yonkers, but ends in Brooklyn and can also carry a billion gallons a day. Part of City Water Tunnel #3 is now open and bringing water to upper Manhattan, the Bronx, and Queens. The last sections of Tunnel #3 are being built in lower Manhattan and Brooklyn.

1936 CITY WATER TUNNEL #2 COMPLETED

1944 DELAWARE RESERVOIRS AND AQUEDUCT COMPLETED

1970 CITY WATER TUNNEL #3 STARTED

2004 CITY WATER TUNNEL #3 ALMOST FINISHED

NOW 1,350,000 000 GALLONS OF WATER COME TO NEW YORK EVERY SINGLE DAY.

11

# Thanks, Gravity

People in NYC don't need to lug their own water home because for almost everyone, gravity brings it to them. The reservoirs of water are upstate in the mountains. The water flows downhill through pipes and tunnels into the city. The water gets moving so fast and builds up such force that it can reach the fifth or sixth story of a tall building with very little help. For taller buildings, there are pumps to push the water up to metal or wooden tanks on the tops of the buildings. Then the water flows down pipes to faucets, toilets, and fire hose connections. Without gravity, water would cost a lot of money because we would have to pay for many more pumps and the power to run them.

water
cable
power
gas
steam

**A**

**subway**

**sewage**

water
distribution
hub

**BEDROCK**

**WATER TUNNEL**

WATER PIPE INTO BUILDING

# bottled or tap?

DRINKING & MESSIN' AROUND

KITCHENS

BATHROOMS

PARKS & GARDENS

FIREFIGHTING

INDUSTRY

New York City has 892 water sampling stations. These stations help to test the water in the pipes underground to see if it's safe to drink. Most of the time, it is. Sometimes, though, particles of dirt and other stuff the water picks up on its trip from the mountains make it cloudy and foul tasting. The city is putting in new filters to make the water taste better. If you want to pay more and forget about gravity, you can always buy your water in bottles.

Water, water, everywhere, Atlantic and Pacific. But New York City's got them beat, Our aqua is terrific!
—Former Mayor Ed Koch

# water in. water out.

NEW YORK CITY ?

AUSTRALIA ?

Some people will try to tell you that water drains from sinks and toilets to the RIGHT in the Southern Hemisphere and to the LEFT in the Northern, but they are wrong. There is something called the Coriolis Effect that is produced by the differences in the speed of the revolving Earth at the poles and the Equator. This effect only changes the directions of big things like cyclones, not small stuff. So the old tale isn't true—water drains in either direction everywhere depending on the shape of the drain and the source of the water.

## LATER, ALLIGATOR

In 1935, an eight-foot-long alligator was captured in a manhole in East Harlem. Nobody knows where it came from, maybe the river, maybe somebody brought a baby alligator home from a trip to Florida and flushed it down the toilet. Are there alligators in the sewers of New York? Nobody knows for sure, but we all sure wonder.

I ♥ NY

# keep your water clean

## super-flush

When everybody flushes their toilet at the same time, like after *American Idol* or when the Superbowl ends, there is a huge drop in the water pressure in the giant tunnels under the city.

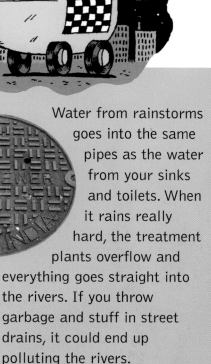

Everything that goes down every drain and toilet in New York City flows through pipes to one of fourteen huge sewage plants. That's 1.4 billion gallons every single day. We know—yuck! Who wants to see that? Or smell it? Surprise! If you go to the swimming pools, skating rink, and sports fields of Riverbank State Park on the West Side Highway between 137th and 145th Streets, you'll be standing right on top of a sewage plant. Under your feet, air, water, and chemicals will be turning sewage into clean water. This way the sewage won't hurt the river or the ocean where it ends up. And because filters and chemicals absorb the odors, the smell isn't bad. Really! Check it out.

Water from rainstorms goes into the same pipes as the water from your sinks and toilets. When it rains really hard, the treatment plants overflow and everything goes straight into the rivers. If you throw garbage and stuff in street drains, it could end up polluting the rivers.

# COMES OUT...

# watertown

**EAST RIVER** The East River, which divides Manhattan and the Bronx from Queens and Brooklyn, isn't a river at all. It's really part of the Atlantic Ocean that connects with Long Island Sound.

**BRONX RIVER** The Bronx River is the last real fresh-water river running on the surface in all of New York City.

**MINETTA BROOK** If you go to the sidewalk in front of 2 Fifth Avenue in Greenwich Village, you will be standing right above Minetta Creek, which now runs underground.

A BROOK WINDS ITS ERRATIC WAY BENEATH THIS SITE
THE INDIANS CALLED IT MANETTE OR DEVIL'S WATER
TO THE DUTCH SETTLERS IT WAS
BESTEVAER'S KILLETJE OR GRANDFATHER'S LITTLE CREEK
FOR THE PAST TWO CENTURIES FAMILIAR TO THIS NEIGHBORHOOD
**MINETTA BROOK**

**SALT MARSHES** Salt marshes are great places to live if you're a fish, bird, or other critter because there's plenty to eat and drink, and lots of places to hide out. But when people build cities they fill in or pollute salt marshes. See what you can save if you try, by visiting the restored marsh at Marine Park in Brooklyn or check out ww.saltmarshalliance.org.

**Even puddles have their fans.**

# water Heroes of NYC

For four hundred years, people dumped industrial waste, toxic chemicals, and all their raw sewage into the rivers without any treatment at all. By 1950, New York's Hudson and East Rivers looked pretty bad.

Pete Seeger, a famous musician, decided that enough was enough. He built a sailboat, the *Clearwater*, and sailed it to Washington, D.C., to demand that the government pass new laws to protect all the country's rivers. The *Clearwater* became a symbol of what people working together can do to clean up and protect the environment. Pete Seeger's boat is still around, taking kids and other volunteers on cruises and helping to keep the rivers healthy and beautiful. You can find out more at www.clearwater.org.

**Andrew Willner** has been an artist, a sea captain, and a boat builder but now he has his dream job. He is New York's Baykeeper. His mission is to make sure people do their best to take care of the precious Hudson estuary and everything connected to it. He has a Web site at www.nynjbaykeeper.org that tells you how you can help him.

**You**, too, can become a Water Hero of New York City. Just look on the next page and get busy.

**New York City is learning to use less water. The average daily water use per New Yorker:**

# WHAT **YOU** CAN DO

1. **PLAY A GAME** How much water can you save with a broom, a toothbrush, a tuna fish can, and a shovel? Find out at www.wateruseitwisely.com.

2. **TAKE A QUIZ** Figure out how much water you use every day taking baths and showers, brushing your teeth, and washing the dishes at nyc.gov/html/dep/pdf/workbook.page8.pdf.

3. **CALCULATE** how much water is wasted by a leak in one of your faucets or toilets at www.awwa.org/advocacy/learn/conserve/dripcalc.cfm.

4. **DO AN EXPERIMENT** that will show you how the water cycle works at www.groundwater.org/kc.activity1.html.

5. **FIND OUT** what the government is doing to help you keep water clean and healthy for you and other living things at www.epa.gov/students/water.htm.

6. **LEARN** more about the ocean at ology.amnh.org/marinebiology/index.html.

7. **NEVER, EVER** throw oil, paint, or other nasty stuff in street drains.

8. **SING SHORTER SHOWER SONGS**, take shallower baths, and don't run the water while you're brushing your teeth.

**NO. 8: Sing Shorter Shower Songs.**

1993: 187 gallons     1997: 165 gallons     2001: 154 gallons     2003: 137 gallons

# NYC ROCKS!

**WELCOME ABOARD.** Every minute of every day, you are taking one of the most amazing rides on Earth. And you don't need a MetroCard. The ground under your feet looks solid, but the rocks are rolling all the time. They move only about an inch between your birthdays, even slower than a school bus in a traffic jam, but it's been happening for most of Earth's 4.6-billion-year history. The rocky crust of our planet is five to twenty miles thick. It is broken into 15 big pieces called plates that are floating on top of red-hot liquid rock called magma. The moving plates crash into each other, and some of the rock dives back down into the magma. New rock comes out of huge rips in the bottom of the ocean. In New York City, you are standing on the North American plate. It is steadily moving west. If you stand in Times Square for two hundred or three hundred million years, you'll end up where Seattle is now.

## WHAT'S ON YOUR PLATE?

**PLATES OF THE WORLD**
1. Pacific
2. Juan de Fuca
3. North American
4. Caribbean
5. Cocos
6. Nazca
7. South American
8. Scotia
9. African
10. Eurasia
11. Arabian
12. Indian
13. Indo-Australian
14. Philippine
15. Antarctica

## TAKE A ROCKY TOUR OF THE BIG APPLE

Rocks are very old and there are lots of different kinds. There are pebbles and gravel and stones that you see all over the place. They have been broken up by wind, water, and ice over thousands of years, or jackhammers and dynamite last week. The real crust of the Earth, though, is called bedrock, and you have to know what to look for. Keep reading, and we'll show you how to spot bedrock in New York City.

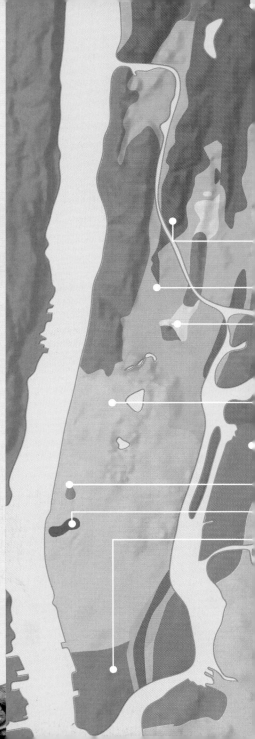

# Welcome to Bedrock

- Yonkers gneiss
- Fordham gneiss
- Inwood marble
- Waloomsac schist
- Hartland formation
- Ravenswood granodiorite
- Serpentine
- Granite
- Manhattan schist

**GNEISS** The oldest bedrock under New York City is more than a billion years old. It is black and white and its name is gneiss (sounds like *nice*). If you want to see lots of it, the gneiss is nice in the northern forest of Van Cortlandt Park in the Bronx or on Roosevelt Island in the East River.

**SCHIST** There is a lot of schist (rhymes with *list*), too. It is about a half billion years old and colored black with silvery flakes. Most of it is underground, but you can go schist hunting on the surface in Morningside Heights, Washington Heights, and Sugar Hill.

**SERPENTINE** Staten Island is mostly made of a kind of rock called serpentine, and you can see plenty of it from the Staten Island Expressway. This rock is green and shiny, so naming it after serpents seemed like a good idea to somebody a long time ago. Serpentine is made from a bunch of other kinds of rocks that got heated up and stuck together as the tectonic plates crashed into each other for hundreds of millions of years.

**MARBLE** Marble is pretty soft compared with rocks like schist and gneiss. It's hard to find on the surface because it gets worn away by wind and water. Marble is beautiful, shimmering white. Workers building subways and tunnels get the best look at it, but you can find big pieces in fields in Harlem.

**HARTLAND ROCKS** When tectonic plates are rumbling around, rocks sometimes get jumbled together. If you want to see some very mixed-up rocks, take a ride on the carousel in Central Park. As you spin around, you'll see great big dark humps everywhere. They are made of gneiss, schist, and other kinds of rocks crushed together.

**THE ICE STOPPED HERE.**

**Look what the glacier left: A building-size boulder sits at Bennett Avenue near West 181st Street in Manhattan.**

# ice COMES TO

And now, the weather report for a nice day in New York City 28,000 years ago...

It's going to get cold. Very cold. Very, very, very cold. For a long, long time.

And it did. The Earth got so cold, in fact, that a 300-foot-thick sheet of ice moved down from the North Pole to near where Flatbush Avenue is now. It covered most of Manhattan and the Bronx and carved out huge grooves in the bedrock. One of them is now the Hudson River. You can also see the grooves in the rocks in Central Park and other big rocks around town. You can sit in one of the grooves and pretend you are a million tons of ice. About 14,000 or 15,000 years ago, the Earth warmed up again and the ice melted. Fast.
It made so much water that it broke through the narrows between what are now Staten Island and Brooklyn and created a beautiful harbor. The melting ice also left a 500-foot-high pile of rocks and gravel called a terminal moraine (sounds like more rain). The terminal moraine marks the place where the ice stopped advancing. It runs from Staten Island across Brooklyn and Queens and continues

# FLATBUSH

east on Long Island. You can still see it's a long, low mountain that was made by rocks and gravel pushed down by the ice. That's why we have neighborhoods with names like Bay Ridge, Park Slope, Crown Heights, and Forest Hills. Humans arrived in the place we now call New York for the first time after the ice left. So did saber-tooth tigers and giant elephant-like animals called mammoths and mastodons. Life got very interesting.

FLATBUSH AVE.

BUS

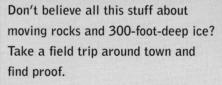

Don't believe all this stuff about moving rocks and 300-foot-deep ice? Take a field trip around town and find proof.

Hint, hint, hint: All of the places in these pictures are evidence that rocks move, and ice covered most of New York City. This chapter has clues about where they are. Can you name them?

4. **Brooklyn Heights: top of the terminal moraine**

3. **Verrazano Narrows bridge over the New York Harbor, which was created when an ice dam broke and caused a huge flood**

2. **Flatbush Avenue, Brooklyn, southern edge of the ice sheet**

1. **Ice-made grooves in Central Park**

# rocks in the sky

You can't get away from rocks in New York City. From just about anywhere, you can see the great rocks of the Empire State Building rising above Midtown Manhattan. Like all skyscrapers, it has a steel skeleton, but its skin is made of granite and limestone. These rocks, like most used for building things, come from pits in the ground called quarries. The rock is cut out of the quarry in blocks and slabs with special saws. Some of the earliest buildings in New York were built of a soft kind of rock called sandstone. It is easier to cut than the harder granite or marble. A lot of the sandstone came from quarries in New Jersey, where it was brown. That's why we call those buildings brownstones. The skins of buildings can also be glass, which is made from ground-up rocks such as quartz. Plenty of buildings are built of brick. There are lots of kinds and sizes of bricks, but all of them are baked clay, not hard rock like granite or marble. Take a look at the pictures on this page, then walk around town and see how many kinds of rocks you can identify.

**FROM TOP: bricks, terra cotta, limestone, and glass**

**CLAYME TO FAME** The question is, da-ta-daaaa...What is the smallest kind of rock?

The answer: clay.

It looks like mud or goo, but Professor Allen Gilbert says clay is made of tiny, tiny bits of rock that are like "the crumbs at the bottom of a potato chip bag." Allen is an anthropologist at Fordham University who studies, among other things, buildings. He explains that the reason there are so many brick buildings in New York City is that there was a big fire in 1835 that burned down 674 wooden buildings. Bricks are made of baked clay, and they don't burn. So, after the terrible fire, people were willing to spend the extra money to buy bricks. Fortunately, there were huge banks of clay along the Hudson River and plenty of trees to fire the ovens to bake the bricks. The Great New York Brick Rush lasted almost a hundred years, and you can still see the results all over town.

# GO CLIMB A ROCK

Central Park is the place to go for learning to climb city rocks. It's called "bouldering," which means safely climbing rocks using just your hands and feet, no ropes. Check out these rocky playgrounds, but make sure it's OK with your grown-ups first.

**Rat Rock i**s on the north edge of the Heckscher Playground near 59th Street just south of the big softball field.

**Chess Rock** is north of Wollman Rink right near the Plaza Hotel (DO NOT climb the hotel!).

**Cat Rock** is an overhang directly north of Wollman Rink and east of Chess Rock. A good spot for winter bouldering.

**Strawberry Boulder Field** is just over the fence at 73rd Street & Central Park West. One boulder is five feet into the park, and more are just down the hill along the horse trail.

**The Ramble**, just north of the Boat Pond, has lots and lots of rocks to climb and is one of the wildest places in New York City.

**Worthless Boulder**, also known as Rap Rock, is on the north edge of the park.

**Lasker Rock**, also known as Harlem Boulder, is just southeast of Worthless Boulder at about 105th Street.

For more hot tips on rock climbing in New York City, go to www.climbnyc.com.

**LEFT AND ABOVE RIGHT: Rat Rock; ABOVE LEFT: Cat Rock**

# Everybody needs a rock collection

Hunting rocks is a lot of fun because they don't bite. A great place to search for rocks is at the beach, but any place where there are a lot of pebbles will do. Just scoop up a handful, then compare them with the pictures on this page. Bingo! You're a geologist.

1. Sandstone
2. Quartzite
3. Marble
4. Shale
5. Limestone
6. Granite
7. Slate
8. Schist
9. Gneiss

# shake rattle & roll

If you're really interested in earthquakes, you'd better get your folks to move to California or someplace else where there are a lot of them. The reason some places—like New York City—don't have many earthquakes is that they are not built near the edges of tectonic plates. Remember? Those plates are always moving. That's where most earthquakes happen. The last big quakes in New York City were more than a hundred years ago. Geologists are pretty sure that a big one will happen again, they're just not sure when—or how much damage it will cause.

## EVERYONE HAS THEIR FAULTS

In some places, called fault lines, you can see where the moving plates tore the city's bedrock crust apart a long time ago. There are many fault lines crisscrossing New York City. In Manhattan, just north of 125th Street, you can see a fault line from the comfort of a subway car. Just take the 1 or the 9 train, and when you get to the 125th Street stop, you'll be aboveground for a moment—and smack in the middle of a fault.

normal fault          thrust fault          strike-slip fault

rocks + sand + humus = DIRT

* Want to make dirt without sand? No worries. Most combos of these three things make dirt.

# let's make dirt

Earth really isn't a good name for our planet because there isn't much earth, meaning dirt, on it. Most of our globe is rock and magma with a thin layer of the stuff we call dirt on the very top. So where does dirt come from? Most of it is rocks that have been broken into tiny bits by ice, snow, rain, and wind over millions of years. Some of it is rocks that have been broken up in the oceans and rivers to become sand. But the best part of dirt is humus. It's formed from decaying animals, the poop of living animals, and dead plants. Humus is the key ingredient of dirt since it helps to grow food. We wouldn't be here without it.

# Worms: heroes of the earth

The next time you're fishing and somebody tells you to put a worm on a hook to trick a fish, think about this: All the humus on Earth has been through a worm or some other creepy critter before it became dirt. Worms, insects, bacteria, and fungi all take in decaying plants and animals and leave humus behind. Chemicals in humus, such as nitrogen, grow the food that all animals, including us, eat. No worms, no burgers.

WILD EXPERIMENT

**GET YOUR FRESH HUMUS HERE!**

### BUILD A WORM BIN

Setting up a worm bin is easy. All you need is a plastic box, damp newspaper strips, some food waste, and common red worms.

Get the worms from a garden store or a bait shop. Put the worms in the box. Add apple peelings, lettuce that got too wilted before you could eat it, leaves, potato skins, and stuff like that. Every day, you can check the worm bin and see that your heroes have made more dirt. When you get enough humus, use it to grow plants in pots or your garden. They'll love it. So will your worms. For help making a worm bin, check out the New York City Compost Project on the Web at www.nyccompost.org.

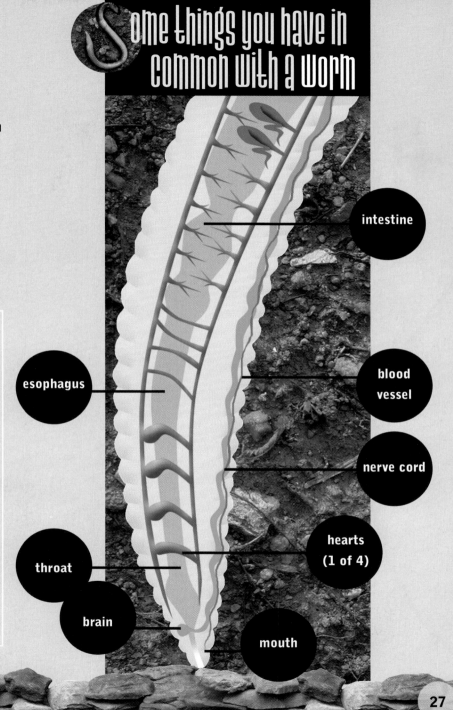

## Some things you have in common with a worm

- intestine
- esophagus
- blood vessel
- nerve cord
- throat
- hearts (1 of 4)
- brain
- mouth

# TAKE A DEEP BREATH

**REALLY.** East Side, West Side, all around the town, you're surrounded by smoke, fumes, and, happily, the atmosphere of Planet Earth. Without the atmosphere, you wouldn't be walking around in New York or any-place else, for that matter. Animals like us need oxygen to stay alive, and the atmosphere has it. We breathe in oxygen and give off carbon dioxide, but those aren't the only gases going back and forth in the atmosphere these days. As long as there were animals and plants keeping the atmos-phere humming along, everything was fine except for the occasional volcano or giant forest fire, and those can't be controlled. Since we humans have been driving cars, building cities, and burning things, the atmosphere has had to deal with other kinds of gases, too. Those gases are called pollution. Pollution makes it harder to breathe, causes all kinds of lung diseases like asthma, and generally stinks. Pollution stays in the air for a long time. It also settles on oceans, forests, and farms, and it's not good for them. Worse yet, human-made pollution is tearing up parts of the atmosphere, such as ozone, that pro-tect Earth from ultraviolet rays in space. Without ozone, the deadly rays can get through to you. Check out Smog City at www.smogcity.com for more proof.

## THE ATMOSPHERE

thermosphere 300+ miles up

mesosphere 50 miles up

stratosphere 30 miles up

ozone layer

troposphere 10 miles up

Earth

**WHAT'S IN AIR?**
nitrogen 78.1%

oxygen 20.9%

argon 0.9%
carbon dioxide 0.1%
and teeny bits
of a lot of other
gases.

## Why is the sky blue? How about **brown?**

Light from the sun reaches Earth as waves of electricity and magnetism. And every color is made by a different kind of visible wave. The waves of blue light are the weakest, so when they hit Earth's atmosphere they scatter all over the place. Unlike blue, the waves of other colors come right on through the atmosphere. The sky is blue because when you look at it you are seeing all those scattered blue waves no matter where you look. Smoke, dust, and exhaust fumes are really tiny particles that get in the way of the blue and make the sky look brown or gray. Yeecccccchhhhh!

## what are you?

You are an air-breathing creature. If you're like most people, you take about 12 breaths a minute. That's 720 breaths an hour, 17,280 breaths a day, or more than six million breaths a year. You breathe air in with a pair of awesome pumps in your chest called lungs. Your lungs send the oxygen from the air into your blood to feed all the cells in your body. After they use the oxygen, the cells send back a gas called carbon dioxide or $CO_2$. When you exhale, or breathe out, your lungs are sending that carbon dioxide back into the atmosphere. Soot, dust, and what comes out of the tailpipes of buses, trucks, and cars ends up in your lungs, which hate New York City traffic worse than you do. Life here and everyplace else on Earth is much harder if the air isn't clean.

# Air today, gone tomorrow?

The big question is how come there's still oxygen in the air after zillions of animals have been breathing it for millions of years. For the answer, go say hello to one of the plants in your home or out in a park. You breathe oxygen and put carbon dioxide back into the atmosphere. Plants take in carbon dioxide and give back oxygen. So, we help each other, and it all works out.

Tree takes dog's carbon dioxide and turns it back into oxygen.

Dog breathes in oxygen

Dog breathes out carbon dioxide

# Take care of the air

The atmosphere will be good to you if you are good to the atmosphere. And we're not doing too bad, really. Seventy-five years ago, the buildings of New York City were black, covered with coal dust, soot, and other pollution. Now, not only do the buildings look better, but so do our lungs. Today, cars, trucks, buses, factories, and everything else that sends gas into our precious atmosphere has to pass tests to be sure it is sending out as little as possible. And people are getting a lot smarter about riding subways, buses, and bikes instead of riding in a car. Just living in the city and not owning a car is a great way to take care of the air. If you have to drive, try carpooling to help prevent more pollution.

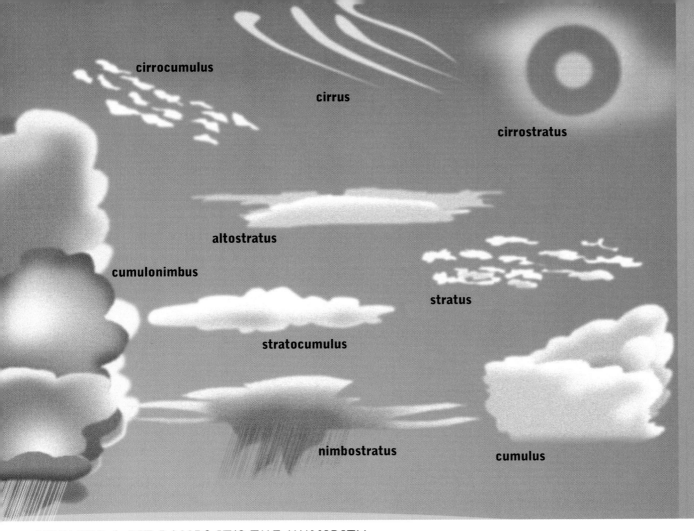

cirrocumulus

cirrus

cirrostratus

altostratus

cumulonimbus

stratus

stratocumulus

nimbostratus

cumulus

There is always water in the atmosphere. Sometimes you can't see it, as when it's a humid August in New York and you're drenched in sweat. Sometimes you can see it, as in the winter when there's steam coming out of a subway grating, or when it's raining or snowing. Clouds are another example of water in the atmosphere that you can see. Clouds form in different shapes depending upon whether the air is hot or cool, still or windy.

## FEELING A BIT DAMP? IT'S THE HUMIDITY.

Humidity is the amount of water vapor in the air. The air picks up moisture as it crosses the continent, and hot air can hold more vapor than cold air. That is why humidity is so bad in the summer in New York City. The higher the humidity number, the more shirts you'll have to change to stay dry.

**AVERAGE RELATIVE HUMIDITY IN NYC IN DEGREES (HIGH/LOW)**

▸ **JAN** 72/60 ▸ **FEB** 70/58 ▸ **MAR** 70/55 ▸ **APR** 68/53 ▸ **MAY** 70/54 ▸ **JUN** 74/58 ▸ **JUL** 77/58 ▸ **AUG** 79/60 ▸ **SEPT** 79/61 ▸ **OCT** 76/57 ▸ **NOV** 75/60 ▸ **DEC** 73/61

# Weather or Climate?

## WHAT'S THE DIFFERENCE?

**Weather** is what's happening in the atmosphere around Brooklyn or the Bronx or wherever your neighborhood is. Raining? Snowing? Windy? Hot? Cold? That's weather. Weather changes all the time because Earth is spinning all the time. The weight of the air, called pressure, changes as the air flows over land and water. It gets hotter or colder and rises or falls, and together that all makes rain, snow, wind, and sunny days.

**Climate** is not weather. Climate is what's happening in very large areas over very long times. For instance, New York City has a climate that is cold in the winter and hot in the summer. So do Moscow, Tokyo, Paris, and other places that are about the same distance from the Equator as New York. The North Pole has a climate that is cold all the time. The Amazon rain forest, near the Equator, has a climate that is hot all the time.

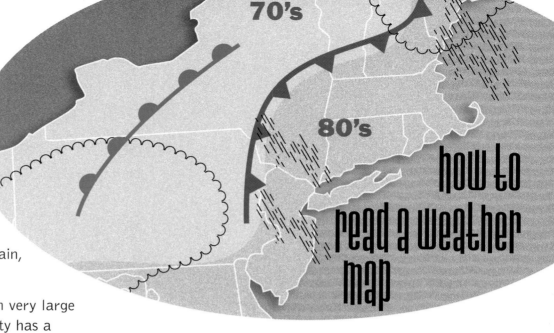

**how to read a weather map**

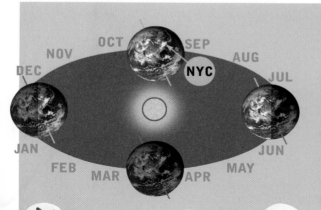

**WINTER, SPRING, SUMMER, FALL** The seasons change because the Earth is tilted on its axis. As our planet moves in its orbit, places get closer or farther away from the sun, causing changes in temperature.
Closer = hotter = summer.
Farther = colder = winter.

The weather arrives in New York from the west after its trip across the continent, but it doesn't have to take a cab into town from the airport. It's hard to know exactly what the weather is going to do when it hits the city. If you can read the symbols on the weather map in the newspaper, your predictions will be almost as good as the TV weather report.

 **COLD FRONTS** are lines where cold air is pushing away warm air. After a cold front passes, the weather is usually cooler and drier.

 **WARM FRONTS** are lines where warm air is pushing away cold air. After a warm front passes, the weather is sometimes milder but often with rain.

 **MOSTLY CLOUDY**

 **SHOWERS**

 **80's** **TEMPERATURE** (in Fahrenheit)

# News Flash : Cities Make Weather!

The next time a thunderstorm soaks you on the way home from school, remember, it might be your own fault. Or your school's fault, because New York and other cities make their own weather. Buildings, concrete, asphalt, cars, trucks, and even millions of people breathing produce heat. The heat rises, hits colder air in the lower atmosphere, makes clouds, and creates rain. Then, because most of the city is covered with pavement, the rain has no place to go. When it finally washes into the lakes and rivers, it carries garbage, oil, and other toxic junk with it. And worse, the heat and pollution from cities is changing the climate as well as the weather on a summer afternoon. There is no question that Earth is getting warmer. And cities are part of the reason.

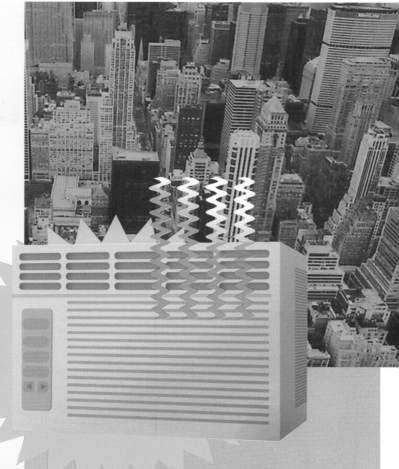

**THE COOLER YOU GET, THE HOTTER IT GETS.**
Huh? True. It's sure something you'll want to think about the next time you turn on an air conditioner. When an air conditioner is working to cool down the inside of your house, it is removing heat and sending it through a vent. That makes the temperature outside a teensy bit hotter, and with millions of air conditioners chugging away at the same time, the temperature outside can get a LOT hotter.

# Extreme New York

**HOTTEST DAY**
July 9, 1936
115 degrees

**COLDEST DAY**
February 9, 1934
−15 degrees

**SNOWIEST DAY**
December 26, 1947
26.4 inches

**RAINIEST DAY**
September 23, 1882
8.28 inches

**WORST HURRICANE**
September 21, 1938
150-mile-an-hour winds

**LAST TORNADO**
October 27, 2003
Staten Island, minor damage

## PROJECT IDEA

### HOT, COLD, WET, DRY, CALM, OR WINDY?
Answer these questions and more every day by making your own weather station. All you need is an empty jar, a can, a strand of hair, chewing gum, and a few other things you can find without leaving your home. Go to www.fi.edu/weather/ to get started.

## AVERAGE TEMPERATURES IN NYC IN FARENHEIT DEGREES

▸ JAN 27.5 ▸ FEB 30.1 ▸ MAR 43.1 ▸ APR 49.8 ▸ MAY 58.7 ▸ JUN 68.3 ▸ JUL 75.8 ▸ AUG 76.7 ▸ SEPT 67.9 ▸ OCT 55.1 ▸ NOV 50.0 ▸ DEC 37.6

# support your local atmosphere

New Yorkers are getting smarter about taking care of the air above them. Since heat is one of the culprits affecting the weather and sending pollution into the atmosphere, it makes sense to keep the buildings from getting too hot on the outside. Roofs that reflect heat are good. So are roofs with gardens, grass, and trees. A nice "green roof" can fool the atmosphere into thinking there's no city there. For more information on green roofs, check out www.greeninggotham.org.

## build a green roof

You'll need some help from your grownups, but if they are in charge of a roof, they can turn it green. All you have to do is make sure the part of the roof you want to make green is waterproof with plastic or a non-poisonous coating. The hard part is hauling dirt up to the roof, but you only have to do it once. You can cover the whole roof with dirt, or just fill a bunch of wooden or metal boxes. Then plant flowers, grass, vegetables, or small trees in the dirt. Don't plant a big tree like a redwood or its roots may end up in your living room.

## WHAT YOU CAN DO

Some pollution comes from dust and smoke from factories and power plants. Power plants are where we get our electricity. Every time you turn on a light from now on, imagine that you are burning gas, oil, or coal and causing pollution. Ask your grown-ups to buy light bulbs that use the least amount of electricity. And for a really good time, go to the emissions calculator at www.airhead.org/Calculator and figure out how much pollution you and everybody else in New York is sending out into our amazing atmosphere.

Want to buy an elevated train track? New Yorkers are trying to raise $40 million to turn the abandoned High Line on Manhattan's West Side into a sky park.

# HEY, NICE PLANTS!

TREES!

FLOWERS!

WEEDS!

POND SCUM!

**IMAGINE THAT IT'S A HOT SUMMER DAY,** and you're walking in Tompkins Square Park in the East Village. Between the dog run and Seventh Street, you see a giant tree with its limbs and dark green leaves covering an area about the size of a soccer field. Under the tree, it's much cooler than in the bright sun. You walk closer and read a sign that says the tree is an American elm more than a hundred years old. You say hello. A dog on a leash swings off the path and says hello to the tree, too, but in a different language. The tree is beautiful, and the shade feels good. But what both you and the dog don't know is that

without this tree and the 2.5 million other trees in New York City, along with other plants, weeds, and even pond scum, neither one of you would be breathing. Trees and plants are nice to look at, but they have a very important job in the Earth's cycle of life. They make oxygen. It's not magic. Trees and plants have stuff called chlorophyll that makes their leaves green. But chlorophyll's most amazing job is to use energy from the sun to convert carbon dioxide from the air into oxygen. You, that dog, and all other air-breathing animals take in oxygen and give out carbon dioxide. In a single year, that one big elm in Tompkins Square Park puts out enough oxygen for a family of four humans breathing every minute of every day. Trees and plants are the lungs of New York City.

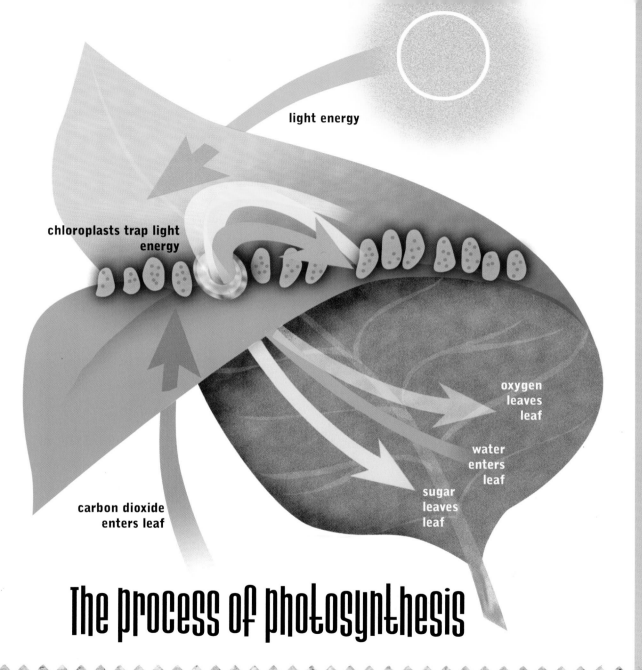

light energy

chloroplasts trap light energy

oxygen leaves leaf

water enters leaf

sugar leaves leaf

carbon dioxide enters leaf

# The process of photosynthesis

# plants take in carbon dioxide, send out oxygen

Chloroplasts in plant cells mix sunlight, carbon dioxide, and water to create the sugars that fuel plant growth and give off oxygen in the process—a neat trick known as photosynthesis.

## PARTS OF A LEAF

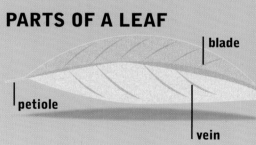

blade

petiole

vein

# Who takes care of trees?

Because trees are so precious to life, New York has an army of workers in the Parks Department who do most of the work of keeping trees healthy. But you can help. Trees in the parks and on city streets need to be trimmed, kept free from diseases that might kill them, and protected from damage by insects. You can learn how to identify trees, check them to see if they're sick, trim branches, and help protect them by becoming a Young Citizen Pruner. To find out how, get in touch with Trees New York at (212) 227-1887 or www.treesny.com.

## PARTS OF A TREE

Leaves collect the sun's energy and make food for the tree. Trees shed their leaves in the winter and move most of their water and sap away from freezing temperatures and into the roots. Some trees, called conifers, have needles instead of leaves. They do the same things with the sun's energy but do not fall off in the winter.

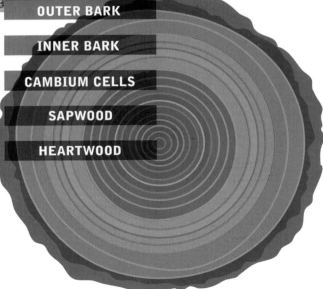

OUTER BARK
INNER BARK
CAMBIUM CELLS
SAPWOOD
HEARTWOOD

## TREENATOMY

The **OUTER BARK** protects the tree.

The **INNER BARK** passes food to the rest of the tree.

The **CAMBIUM CELL LAYER** produces new wood and bark.

The **SAPWOOD** moves water to the leaves.

The **HEARTWOOD** is the main support for the tree.

**I think that I shall never see A poem lovely as a tree.**

**Joyce Kilmer**

# the OLDEST living New Yorker

From the Douglaston Plaza Mall in Queens you can see a giant tulip tree soaring into the sky. It is the tallest and oldest living thing in New York City. When the tree sprouted from its seed about 450 years ago, Queens was a wetland wilderness, and Pilgrims hadn't landed at Plymouth Rock. Now, the champion tree is 135 feet tall and 19 feet around. If you go out to see the Queens Giant, you can learn more about it and the other wonderful life in Alley Pond Park by stopping at the Environmental Center, (718) 229-4000, or www.alleypond.com.

## GROW YOUR OWN TREE TODAY

Take a walk down to the corner fruit stand and buy an avocado. Eat it, but save the seed. Wash the seed. Stick three toothpicks into the seed so you can suspend it on top of a small jar of water with the wide end of the seed down. Put the jar in a warm place but not in direct sunlight. In just a few days, your tree will begin to grow. When it gets to about six inches, cut it back to about three inches. As soon as the leaves come back on top of the stem, plant your tree in rich soil in a 10-inch pot, leaving the top half of the seed exposed. Water often but not too much at a time. If the leaves turn yellow, you're using too much water. The avocado will like living in your house or apartment better than outside. Take care of your tree and watch it grow!

# park yourself in a park

New York City has more than 1,700 parks where trees and plants get the respect they deserve, and people play and relax. Together the parks total 28,000 acres, which is bigger than most whole cities.

**VISIT THE BIG FIVE**
Guess which park at right is the biggest?

1. Pelham Bay Park, Bronx, 2,765 acres
2. Greenbelt, Staten Island, 1,778 acres
3. Flushing Meadows Corona Park, Queens, 1,255 acres
4. Van Cortlandt Park, Bronx, 1,146 acres
5. Central Park, Manhattan, 843 acres

**Flushing Meadows, Queens**

**Central Park, Manhattan**

**Greenbelt, Staten Island**

**Van Cortlandt Park, Bronx**

**Pelham Bay Park, Bronx**

# wild preserves of New York City

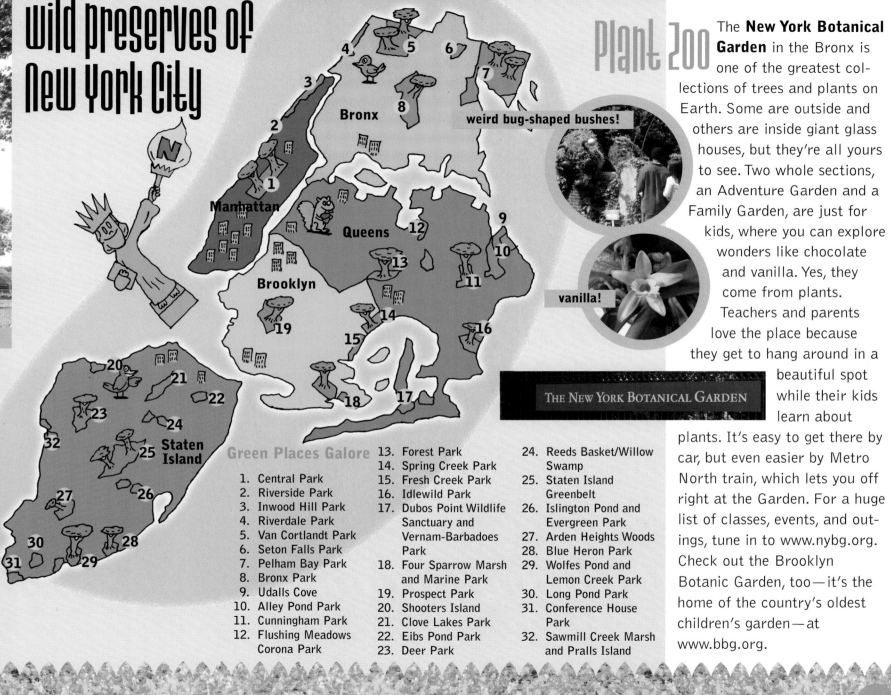

**Bronx**

**Manhattan**

**Queens**

**Brooklyn**

**Staten Island**

weird bug-shaped bushes!

vanilla!

## Plant Zoo

The **New York Botanical Garden** in the Bronx is one of the greatest collections of trees and plants on Earth. Some are outside and others are inside giant glass houses, but they're all yours to see. Two whole sections, an Adventure Garden and a Family Garden, are just for kids, where you can explore wonders like chocolate and vanilla. Yes, they come from plants. Teachers and parents love the place because they get to hang around in a beautiful spot while their kids learn about plants. It's easy to get there by car, but even easier by Metro North train, which lets you off right at the Garden. For a huge list of classes, events, and outings, tune in to www.nybg.org. Check out the Brooklyn Botanic Garden, too—it's the home of the country's oldest children's garden—at www.bbg.org.

THE NEW YORK BOTANICAL GARDEN

## Green Places Galore

1. Central Park
2. Riverside Park
3. Inwood Hill Park
4. Riverdale Park
5. Van Cortlandt Park
6. Seton Falls Park
7. Pelham Bay Park
8. Bronx Park
9. Udalls Cove
10. Alley Pond Park
11. Cunningham Park
12. Flushing Meadows Corona Park
13. Forest Park
14. Spring Creek Park
15. Fresh Creek Park
16. Idlewild Park
17. Dubos Point Wildlife Sanctuary and Vernam-Barbadoes Park
18. Four Sparrow Marsh and Marine Park
19. Prospect Park
20. Shooters Island
21. Clove Lakes Park
22. Eibs Pond Park
23. Deer Park
24. Reeds Basket/Willow Swamp
25. Staten Island Greenbelt
26. Islington Pond and Evergreen Park
27. Arden Heights Woods
28. Blue Heron Park
29. Wolfes Pond and Lemon Creek Park
30. Long Pond Park
31. Conference House Park
32. Sawmill Creek Marsh and Pralls Island

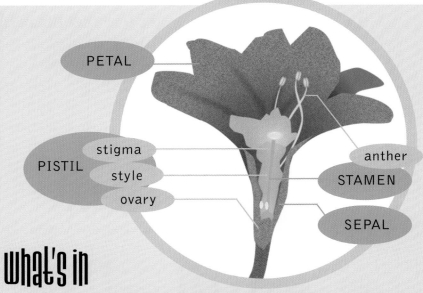

PETAL

PISTIL
- stigma
- style
- ovary

anther
STAMEN

SEPAL

# What's in a flower?

All those cut flowers wrapped in cellophane down at the corner deli aren't there just to make you smile. When they were alive, they were hard at work. Flowers come in thousands of shapes and colors, with one job: to make seeds that make baby plants. But they can't do it alone. Flowers that are big, bright, and fragrant usually get help from bees, birds, and butterflies. Flowers that are small and dull and don't smell very much use the wind. Plants that smell really bad, like the world's biggest plant, the corpse flower, get their help from dung beetles and flies.

**PEEEE-YU!**

**The corpse flower is native to Indonesia and was first on display at the New York Botanical Garden in 1937. Many other gardens have corpse flowers now, and there's always a lot of press coverage when one of them blooms. Keep an eye on the newspapers, and maybe someday you'll get a whiff.**

# City Smells

1. **CHERRY BLOSSOMS**
   Splashy in the early spring.
2. **PINK LADY'S SLIPPER**
   Try one on. Kidding.
3. **POISON IVY**
   Leaves of three, let it be.
4. **CORNER DELI**
   Around the world to your block.
5. **DANDELION**
   Put 'em in your salad.
6. **JAPANESE HONEYSUCKLE**
   Hardy out-of-towner.
7. **WILDFLOWERS**
   Pick up a pack of seeds and scatter them around.
8. **VOODOO LILY**
   Smells kinda like a corpse flower.
9. **ROSE GARDEN**
   Take a sniff.

1 pretty

4 cheap

7 wild

**ALLERGIES = PLANTS IN LOVE**
Bless you. Pollen, which is one of the parts of plants that helps them make new plants, causes allergy nightmares for some people in the spring. It's no wonder you're sneezing.

# New York in Bloom

Have you noticed how many daffodils there are all over town in the spring? After the tragedy of September 11, 2001, volunteer New Yorkers—20,000 of them—planted more than two and a half million daffodils as a living memorial. The Daffodil Project is still going on, and you can become a Daffodil Planter by calling (212) 838-9410 or going to www.ny4p.org.

**INVASIVE SPECIES:** Not all plants are welcome in New York. These unwanted plants are called invasive species, usually fast-growing vines, grasses, and weeds that humans (oops) introduced into the wild, where they crowd out older types of plants.

43

# Grow, grow, grow your own

There aren't any big farms in New York City anymore, but there are hundreds of small ones, and probably at least one within a short walk of where you are right now. Really. New York City has the biggest community garden network in the country! Since 1978, the members of a group called Green Thumb have been turning empty lots into gardens that produce food and flowers and send all that wonderful oxygen back into the atmosphere. The gardens also give people a chance to dig in the dirt; plant seeds that grow into beautiful plants; eat ripe tomatoes, lettuce, onions, and all kinds of other vegetables; and enjoy working together in their neighborhoods. You can find the garden nearest you and get gardening by going to www.greenthumbnyc.org.

# Plant a seed, watch it grow

If gardening wasn't pretty easy, people wouldn't have been doing it for thousands of years. You can buy seeds at hardware and houseplant stores. They come with instructions about how much to water them, whether they like direct or indirect sunlight, and anything else you need to know to grow them. Some gardeners buy seeds that have already sprouted into little plants, called starts, which makes things easier and faster. Sometimes you can buy starts in the spring at green markets in your neighborhood. Whether you are planting your seeds in a window box, pot, or your local public garden, they need four things to grow and live happy lives.

**1. Soil** which contains food to feed the plant through its roots. In public gardens, people often make their own rich soil by mixing compost and other fertilizer with what's there already. In pots and window boxes, you might want to use bags of soil that you buy at hardware and houseplant stores or in the Garden District.

**2. Water,** which comes from the sky or a hose if your plants are outside, or a watering can or a cup if they're inside.

**3. Sunlight,** which comes from, well, you know.

**4. Tender, Loving Care,** which is a lot of fun.

## THE PAYOFF FOR GARDENING IN NEW YORK CITY

**ROOTS:** carrots, beets, radishes, parsnips, turnips

**STEMS:** asparagus, celery, rhubarb, leeks, green onions

**LEAVES:** lettuce, spinach, parsley, cabbage

**FLOWERS:** broccoli, cauliflower, artichokes, nasturtiums

**FRUIT:** tomatoes, apples, cherries, pumpkins

# RULERS OF NEW YORK

**IT'S NIGHTTIME** and you need a drink of water, so you get out of bed, tiptoe barefooted into the kitchen, turn on the light, and SCREAM. There they are, all over the sink, all over the floor, all over the walls. Cockroaches. Brown, skittering, chittering, nasty cockroaches. Pretty soon, everybody in the house is up, but by the time they get to the kitchen, the roaches have disappeared. They're still there, though, hiding and waiting for the right moment to remind you again that New York is *their* city, not yours.

Cockroaches are members of the largest tribe of animals on Earth, the arthropods, which includes insects, spiders, and crabs. Most people just call them bugs. All of them have their skeletons on the outside—or hard shells that most of them have to shed to grow. Scientists have named about a million and a half animals, and one million of them are arthropods. There are thousands of different kinds of bugs in Gotham. Some of them, such as the mites in everybody's eyebrows (yes, you have mites in your eyebrows!!), are so small as to be invisible without a microscope. Others, such as bees, ants, beetles, fireflies, mosquitoes, flies, ladybugs, grasshoppers, dragonflies, and, of course, cockroaches, you see everywhere you look. They're creepy, crawly, and sometimes a little bit scary, but you'll be amazed how many insects are working to make life more pleasant. When you tell your nighttime cockroach story, somebody will probably say, "Oh, yuck. Someday those darn bugs will take over the city."

After reading this chapter, you can tell them that they already have.

# King Cockroach: Up close and personal

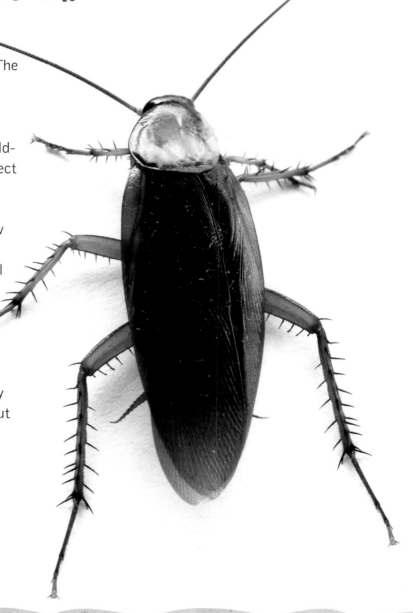

So you aren't crazy about cockroaches, but maybe that's because you don't know them well enough. First of all, they didn't ask to be in New York City. The first cockroaches arrived in North America on ships with European colonists, probably with the Pilgrims on the *Mayflower*, and they never stopped coming. Like tourists with fresh MetroCards, cockroaches love New York. The warm buildings, hot summers, and plenty of places to hide are just perfect for them. Now, there are four different kinds in the five boroughs. The ones that do that disappearing act in the kitchen when the light comes on are German cockroaches. They grow to a little over a half inch long, love damp places like under sinks, and can squeeze through a crack as narrow as a pencil lead. American cockroaches, actually from Africa, can grow to three inches long and live mostly in warm, damp basements, but might show up in your bathroom on a warm, steamy night. Brown-banded cockroaches are smaller than the others and hide out in electrical appliances. And Oriental cockroaches are an inch long and mostly live in garbage dumps. Now that you know a little more about cockroaches, you shouldn't get too cozy with them. German cockroaches can cause a lot of problems for humans. Their poop, skins, and skeletons carry stuff called roach dust that causes allergies, and they are one of the leading causes of asthma among children in cities. Another not-so-nice thing about roaches is that they are very, very hard to get rid of. OK, no matter how well you know them, cockroaches are still revolting.

**EYES** Cockroaches have compound eyes with 2,000 separate lenses that let them see in all directions around their bodies. They can't see too well in red light, but great in green.

**ANTENNAE** Sniff, sniff. Roaches smell with feelers on their heads.

**LEGS** All the better to touch you. Hairs on cockroach legs give them an extra sense of touch.

**CERCI** Roaches have two little hairs on their rear ends that are like motion detectors. That's why it's hard to sneak up on them from behind.

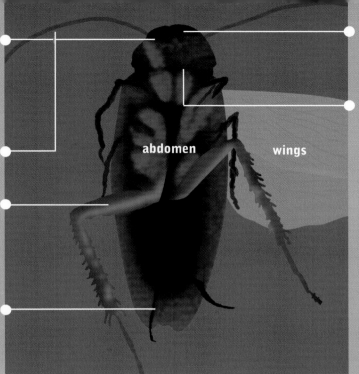

abdomen    wings

**MOUTH** A cockroach mouth can smell as well as taste and moves from side to side instead of up and down.

**SALIVA GLANDS** Cockroaches can spit.

**REPRODUCTION** Cockroaches don't go on dates. Females attract males with an odor. When the female becomes pregnant, she stays so for the rest of her life—laying eggs until she dies.

# CREEPY COCKROACH FACTS

▶ Cockroaches evolved on Earth about 280 million years ago, and they looked just about like they do now.

▶ Cockroaches have 6 legs and 18 knees and can run 3 miles an hour, which means that if one was as big as you are it would be going about 100 mph!

▶ A cockroach can live for a week without its head. Actually, when it loses its head the only reason it dies is because it can't get anything to drink. It can live for a month without food.

▶ A cockroach can hold its breath for 40 minutes.

▶ If you have a stinging wound, like from a bee, just catch a few cockroaches, crush them into mush, and put the mush on your oweee. The stinging will go away, if you can stand mushed-up roaches on you.

# Bugs of New York

1. Praying Mantis
2. Junebug
3. Dung Beetle
4. Damsel Fly

5. Widow Skimmer
6. Firefly
7. Eastern Swallowtail

Beekeeper David Graves

# Don't squash that ant. Its family is watching.

Many insects don't have much of a family life. Their parents lay the eggs and hit the road without even saying good-bye. Some bugs, though, such as ants and bees, hatch and become members of the most organized house-holds in the animal kingdom. The members of a colony usually have the same mother, called, of course, THE QUEEN. And from the minute they hatch from eggs they work all the time to keep the colony safe and alive. These social insects communicate with dancing and different patterns of flight, and their amazing cooperation is one reason bugs rule New York City.

# How sweet is New York?

There's a lot of clover in New York City, and bees love clover. A beekeeper from Massachusetts named David Graves knew that where there were bees there would be honey, so he put some hives on rooftops in Brooklyn, the Bronx, and Manhattan and went into business. Now, bees that live in his hives fly around, pick up flower nectar and pollen from parks, gardens, and flowerpots, and bring it back to make honey. Want some? It's five dollars a jar—find it at the Union Square green market.

**PROJECT IDEA**
**Get yourself an ant farm to watch them up close.**

**MAKE YOUR PARENTS CRAZY.**
Many people in the world eat insects, and you can, too. Stores in New York City sell chocolate-covered bees, caterpillars, and ants, so check the Yellow Pages and put Mom and Dad into shock.

# Bugs = life as we know it

Roaches get a lot of press, but New York is also swarming with insects that work around the clock—like tiny sanitation crews keeping the city clean. Bugs eat decomposing leaves, bark, garbage, and almost everything else that falls to the ground. Bugs are also food, which is not so good for the bugs but great for the birds, frogs, and other critters that eat them. If all the insects on Earth disappeared overnight, life as we know it would cease to exist. Bees, wasps, flies, butterflies, and other insects that pollinate plants would be gone, so there would be no more fruit, vegetables, or flowers. Birds, lizards, frogs, and other animals with insects at the top of their menus would die. And all the dead plants and garbage that insects eat would pile up and make the world a huge, stinking garbage dump. Think of that before you squash a spider or an ant.

## SURPRISE!

The first new species found in Central Park in more than a hundred years is a kind of **centipede.** These creepy crawlers are less than half an inch long. Centipedes look like caterpillars, but they have more legs. Some centipedes are poisonous. The new discovery has 82 legs, lives in rotting leaves, plants, and twigs, and looks a little bit like some Asian centipedes. It probably hitched a ride to New York City in a potted plant.

## BE KIND TO SPIDERS

Most spiders, aka arachnids—which are not, scientifically speaking, insects—use venom to capture their prey, and once in a while a human gets stung. But that's no reason to step on every spider you see. They eat pesky bugs such as flies and mosquitoes and generally keep bug populations from getting too huge.

# Bugs at work

1. Aphids eat plants. Ladybugs eat aphids. Enough said

2. These worker ants carry 50 times their weight, and they are all females

3. Pollen on the back legs is a sure sign of a busy bee

4. Wasps are a pain at picnics but are great pollinators

All those beautiful skeletons you see in natural history museums were cleaned by hard-working bugs. **Dermestid beetles** can clean a large skull in two or three days, and the American Museum of Natural History has a colony of them in the basement. Want a dermestid colony of your own? First, ask your adults. Then, just go to a museum, and the person in charge of bonecleaning will probably be glad to give you a few, or you can buy some at a scientific-supply store. Then just put them in a container big enough to hold the bones you want to clean, feed the beetles a little meat every once in a while when they're not busy, and you're in business.

**Dermestid Beetle**

(actual size)

# They're baaaack!

On an evening in early summer 2004, as the sun was setting over the Hudson, alien invaders rose from holes in the ground. They had waited for 17 years feeding on tree roots underground until it was time to attack. Billions and billions of them flew into the sky together in great swarms sweeping across the East Coast and into the streets and parks of New York City. Relax. They're cicadas, bugs that look like grasshoppers about two inches long, and they're on the move to find mates, not to eat you up. Cicadas are migrating bugs with long growth cycles of 17 years. They make a noise in the sky that sounds like hamburger meat hitting a hot skillet. They are said to taste like boiled asparagus, and they crackle under your feet when you step on them!

Insect invaders can do a lot more damage than just smooshing on the soles of your shoes like cicadas. The **Asian long-horned beetles** can kill trees. They were first found in Greenpoint, Brooklyn, in 1996 after accidentally arriving by ship from China. Now they have colonized Central Park, Flushing Meadows Park, and other city forests. This new arrival has the city on the lookout. To find out what to look for and how to help get rid of them, go to www.nyc govparks.org.

Another tree-eater, the **gypsy moth**, showed up in New York City in 1922, and it's still around, even though some of the deadliest (to humans) pesticides were used to stop it.

# How far? How high?

If you are on the observation deck of the Empire State Building and notice a fly buzzing around your head, don't be surprised. A fly can easily reach the thousand feet you climbed by fast elevator, and some butterflies have been spotted at altitudes up to 20,000 feet.

# Bug magic

## Want some good news?

All bug invasions are not disasters. Every autumn, for instance, beautiful monarch butterflies make their journey from the northeastern United States to the forests of Mexico. On their way, the monarchs spend a few days in New York City, seeing shows, going dancing...not really. They land in Clove Lakes Park on Staten Island, Central Park in Manhattan, and other places around town to rest up and lay eggs. To get in on the welcoming party, join New York's annual Monarch Watch at www.monarchwatch.org.

Monarch caterpillar (left) and butterfly (below)

CANADA

UNITED STATES

MEXICO

NYC

and winter migration paths (map)

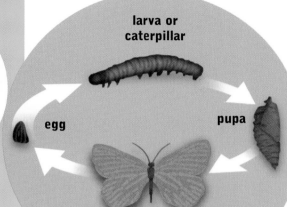

larva or caterpillar

egg

pupa

adult butterfly

## Many insects

change their outer bodies in a process called metamorphosis. The word comes from Greek for "transformation," and that's just what happens. A butterfly, for instance, begins life as an egg on a leaf, and in a week, a caterpillar (larva) eats its way out of the egg. For two or three weeks, the caterpillar eats the leaf and then wraps itself in a silk cocoon attached to a twig called a pupa. About ten days later, it breaks out of the cocoon as a butterfly.

# FUR, FINS, FANGS, & FEATHERS

**JUST A HUNDRED YEARS AGO,** horses, pigs, sheep, and cattle shared the streets of New York City with the humans who were supposedly in charge. Since there were so many critters roaming around, not many people had house pets. Now, though, millions of dogs, cats, fish, and other pets practically run the lives of their humans. They take you for walks, make you buy them food and litter, curl up on your bed and snore, and complain if they don't get enough attention. But everybody loves them. There are about 100,000 licensed dogs throughout the five boroughs, but probably 500,000 without licenses. Nobody knows for sure how many pet cats, snakes, turtles, hamsters, fish, and potbellied pigs there are, but it's a pretty good bet that they outnumber all the humans in New York City.

## City Pets

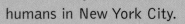

56

## Zoo York City

New York is a big city where people can feel cut off from nature. Sometimes, they try to feel closer to the natural world by bringing "nature" home with them.

In the fall of 2003, a Harlem man was arrested for keeping a 400-pound tiger and a 4-foot alligator in his five room apartment. The tiger had attacked him. Wild animals shouldn't live in apartments; it's cruel to the animals and dangerous for everyone around them. It's also illegal.

Zoos provide animals with safe, stimulating environments where they can be cared for properly. When you feel the desire to experience the wild, go to www.bronxzoo.com and plan a visit.

# Take a walk on the wild side

If you're walking down Broadway, chances are pretty slim that you'll see any wild animals except maybe birds, squirrels, a rat or two, and your little sister. In the parks, marshes, and open fields of New York City, though, you might just run into a coyote, skunk, white-footed mouse, opossum, raccoon, or muskrat. The best time to scout for your furry wild neighbors is in the early morning or the evening. If you do spot one and want to tell the world, go to http://urbanneighbors.nypl.org and look for the Wildlife Sighting Log.

## Sharpen your tracking skills

### WHOSE FEET MADE THESE TRACKS?

1. CHIPMUNK
2. MUSKRAT
3. OPOSSUM
4. HUMAN
5. RACCOON
6. WOODCHUCK
7. EASTERN COTTONTAIL
8. EASTERN COYOTE

**1**

**4**

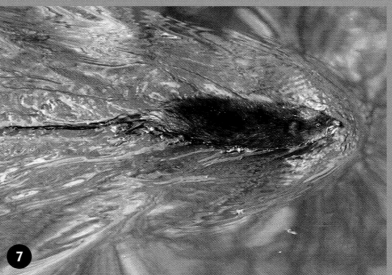

**WHO'S WHO?**
1. Coyote
2. Opossum
3. Chipmunk
4. Eastern Cottontail
5. Raccoons
6. Skunks
7. Muskrat

# Rat–Squirrel Smackdown

**And now, for the main event in the Wild New York battle for the furry critter championship**

**On the left,** King Rat, familiar to you all from lucky sightings down on the subway tracks, in stations, alleys, and in damp, dark places of every kind. His aliases include brown rat and Norway rat, but for most people, a rat is a rat is a dirty rat. New York is rat heaven. Nobody knows exactly how many rats there are in New York City, but estimates range from 44 million to 96 million. "We don't do tail counts," said one city official, "but there are a lot of them." The first rats probably got to New York during the American Revolution, and though people have been trying to get rid of them ever since, they're still here. When the Americans were testing A-bombs on Pacific islands, the only creatures left alive after the blasts were rats. One mother rat can have 150 rat pups in a year, and each of those pups will grow up to have jaws that can bite down with 20,000 pounds of pressure per square inch, enough to break the lock on your bicycle. One word: Yikes!

**On the right,** our local hero, Skippy the Squirrel. OK, OK. A squirrel is a rodent, just like a rat, but this guy, aka the eastern gray squirrel, is actually a New York City native. Its ancestors were living happily in the undisturbed forests along the Hudson and on Long Island long before people got here. Then, each squirrel needed about one acre—about half of Union Square Park—to have enough food to survive. These days, the living is easier for squirrels because people and garbage feed them as well as the trees, and there are more than 20 squirrels per acre of open space. There are about 28,000 acres of parks in the five boroughs, so...well, you do the math. Either way, let's just say that squirrels may be the sentimental favorite, but rats are winning the numbers game—by about 100 to 1.

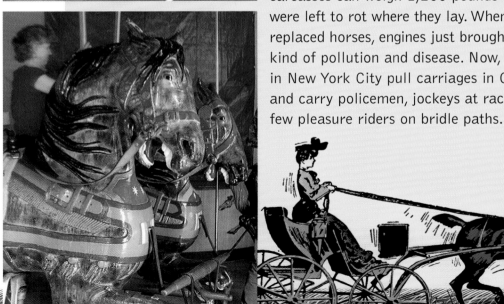

# City of horses

At the end of the 19th century, there were 150,000 horses living on Manhattan Island alone. The streets were full of them, along with constant clipping and clopping, whips cracking, snorting and neighing, not to mention everything they left behind, which caused all kinds of diseases. Each horse in New York City dropped 24 pounds of manure and several quarts of pee every day. Even though all these horses and other animals filled the city, there was no systematic street cleaning. During the winter, streets and sidewalks were sometimes covered with several feet of hardened animal waste and snow. The reason many houses have stoops and their main entrances on the second floor is to rise above the manure. And worse, horses died all the time. Since their carcasses can weigh 1,200 pounds or more, many were left to rot where they lay. When the automobile replaced horses, engines just brought a different kind of pollution and disease. Now, the only horses in New York City pull carriages in Central Park and carry policemen, jockeys at racetracks, and a few pleasure riders on bridle paths.

# City Slimeballs

One thing you never have to worry about in New York City is getting bittem by a wild poisonous snake. The last of them, timber rattlesnakes, were driven out of the Bronx by streets, buildings, and people with pitchforks and guns. Snakes generally avoid people, but if you're lucky you still might see a garter snake in a park. You DO have to worry about getting bitten by another kind of reptile if you dip your toe into the wrong pond at the wrong time. Snapping turtles have been around since the time of the dinosaurs, and they're still here. These things are amazing. They can grow to weights of 40 pounds or more. They have survived the past four centuries in New York City. And nearly every lake or pond in every borough has at least one snapping turtle lurking in its depths.

An even older New Yorker is the horseshoe crab, which is not really a crab. It is more closely related to spiders. You have to go to the beach or a mudflat to see one, but it's worth the trip. Every spring between mid-May and mid-June, thousands of these fierce-looking but harmless creatures crawl from the sea to mate and lay eggs on Brooklyn's Manhattan Beach. Horseshoe crabs are very cool and spooky—and they've been on Earth for around 1.2 billion years.

Eastern Garter Snake

Clam

Horseshoe Crab

Snapping Turtle

**Most waters** around New York have fish, too. There are great fishing spots in Clove Lakes Park, Hudson River Park, Jones Beach, and dozens of other places inside the city limits. In New York, the best time for fishing is in late summer and fall. In fresh water, you can catch bass, perch, and crappie, and in salt water, bluefish, striped bass, and even tuna near the Verrazano Narrows Bridge. Here's the bad news. Even though estuaries, rivers, ponds, and streams are cleaner now, they still contain pollutants that are harmful to kids under 15 years old, so the health department says you shouldn't eat what you catch in the waters of New York City. Besides, it's better to send that fish back home for another day in the wild. For more information about the fish of New York City and how you can help make them safer to eat, go to www.riverkeeper.org.

**Brook Trout**

**Bullfrog**

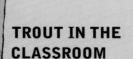

### TROUT IN THE CLASSROOM

Catching fish with a hook and line isn't the only way to get to know them. There's the New York Aquarium with thousands of fish from all over the world (www.nyaquarium.com). You can also set up your own aquarium with help from fish stores all over the place, and if you really want to study our finny friends, get your grown-ups to join up with Trout in the Classroom. They have trout-growing programs in almost a hundred New York City schools and would love to start one in yours. Just go to www.troutinthe classroom.com to get started.

Jamaica Bay

**Seabirds**

**Birds of Prey**

**Shore and Wading Birds**

**Waterfowl (ducks and geese)**

THE BIG APPLE

# Boid is the woid

Tourists fly into LaGuardia and JFK in swarms, but their numbers can't compare with the migrating birds that wing their way into town every year. New York City is one of the main rest stops on the Atlantic Coast Flyway, a bird superhighway that runs from breeding grounds in northeastern Canada to warmer winter homes in the Caribbean and South America. Pigeons, hawks, seagulls, and many of the other birds you see around the city are permanent residents who like tall buildings and garbage, but waves of visitors come through at different times of the year. Get out your bird books and in spring look for warblers, Baltimore orioles (not the baseball team), wood thrushes, and other migrating songbirds all over the city. In summer you'll see full-timers like cardinals, sparrows, and starlings, and in fall, look for hawks, falcons, ducks and geese, and even bald eagles.

To birds, Central Park is a big green target from above, so it's a great place for watching the migrating flocks. Some sharp-eyed bird-watchers have seen more than 100 types of birds in the park in a single day. Another bird favorite is the huge Jamaica Bay Wildlife Refuge in southern Queens and Brooklyn. The birds fly thousands of miles to get there, some navigating by the stars, others following landmarks, but you can just buy a MetroCard and take the A train.

**A peregrine falcon can fly more than 9,000 miles from Greenland to Uruguay, and back. But some stay year-round in NYC.**

**Great Blue Heron**

**Hooded Merganser**

**Screech Owl**

**Great Egret**

# how to watch birds

With your eyes, of course. A good pair of binoculars helps, too, and...

▸ Get a bird book to figure out what to look for and where to look.

▸ Go bird-watching with somebody who's done it before.

▸ Walk softly through the park forest and listen for birdcalls.

▸ Keep a checklist of the birds you see and try to remember their voices.

▸ Set out a feeder and let the birds come to you.

**Believe it or not, bird watching is the number one out-of-the-house activity for Americans. And, lucky you, New York City is one of the best places in the country to do it.**

For a list of birds you can see right now in NYC, go to the Prospect Park Audubon Society Web site at www.prospect parkaudubon.org.

**Black-capped Chickadee**

**Pigeons (duh)**

**House Finch**

**Redtail Hawk**

65

# FOOD IN, GARBAGE OUT
## Time to feed the people

**EVERY TIME YOU ORDER A MEAL** in a restaurant, call for takeout, fill up your basket at a grocery store, or grab an orange at a corner fruit stand or green market, you are part of the 20-billion-dollar-a-year business of feeding the humans in New York City. That's a lot of food! Where does all that food come from? How did it get here? And what happens to the orange peels, potato skins, bones, paper, plastic, and the rest of the garbage when you're finished eating?

**RESTAURANT AND TAKE OUT**
$11,183,055,000

**FRUIT AND VEGETABLES**
$1,603,332,000

**SEAFOOD**
$412,304,000

**MEAT AND POULTRY**
$1,352,528,000

**PACKAGED/ FROZEN FOOD**
$1,527,319,000

**BAKED GOODS**
$1,853,289,000

**DAIRY/EGGS**
$2,014,307,000

**YUM**
From falafel to sushi, the entire world provides the buffet that New Yorkers call lunch.

# The long road to lunch

Until the middle of the 19th century, just about everything New Yorkers ate came from within walking distance of where they lived. That's still true in many parts of the world, but if it were true in New York City today, squirrels, pigeons, and food from small gardens would be at the top of everybody's menus. Now, the things you put in your mouth in New York City travel an average of 1,300 miles to get to town, and some of it, such as lettuce, tomatoes, and other produce in the winter, comes from the Southern Hemisphere, where it's summer. This food makes its way to New York by plane, boat, and truck trips of 5,000 or 6,000 miles. That means that, if those planes, boats, and trucks aren't running, or if fuel costs soar, or if there are hurricanes, droughts, crop diseases, or other problems that you never even hear about, that banana, potato, or broccoli might not make it to your table.

## I'D LIKE TO ORDER SOME TAKEOUT, PLEASE

When you call up to order a nice take-out lunch, the mixed vegetable tofu that arrives with chopsticks and hot sauce will have made a heck of a trip. The tofu might have been made from soybeans grown in Chile. The vegetables, perhaps from California, come to New York by truck or train to a huge food distribution center like the one at Hunts Point in the Bronx. From there, a smaller truck takes them to the local restaurant, and then, finally, the guy on a bike brings them to your door.

# Eat local, take care of your farmer

If you don't want to be at the end of a food chain that involves thousands of miles, and trucks, trains, and planes, which all send pollution into the air, you can buy food at a green market. There are 42 green markets in the 5 boroughs that sell only food produced near New York City. The bonus is that your meat and produce are thousands of miles fresher. You can take a guided tour of the largest green market in Union Square and meet the farmers on Monday, Wednesday, or Friday. You can also get a list of all the green markets in New York City and the farms that supply them at www.farmtotable.org.

▶ There are 42 markets in 31 locations in Manhattan, Brooklyn, Queens, the Bronx, and Staten Island.

▶ More than 250,000 customers frequent the markets every week in peak season.

▶ More than 105 restaurants obtain ingredients from Greenmarket farmers each week.

▶ Greenmarket farmers donate about 500,000 pounds of food to City Harvest and other hunger relief organizations each year.

# Want to know something gross?

New York City's humans produce enough garbage every day to fill up the Empire State Building. That's over 9,000 tons, enough to fill 550 semitrailer trucks that would form a line on the highway 9 miles long. That's a lot of garbage, and it all has to go somewhere. So where do they take it? The city has been churning out garbage for several centuries now, and the dumps are full. One of them, the Fresh Kills Landfill on Staten Island, is so big that it can be seen from space. Fresh Kills was closed in 2001, so now most of the garbage goes on trucks and barges to dumps in New Jersey, Pennsylvania, and Virginia.

## FIND OUT WHERE YOU STAND

Every paper towel, every orange peel, every plastic bottle, everything else you use every day makes garbage. To find out how much, go to NYC WasteLe$$ at www.nycwasteless.org and take the quiz.

## How much garbage does NYC make?

Yard waste 4% 381.48 tons

Metals 5% 476.85 tons

Other 21% 2002.77 tons

Rubber, leather, textiles 6% 572.22 tons

Plastics 10% 953.70 tons

Glass 6% 572.22 tons

Paper and paperboard 33% 3147.21 tons

Food 15% 1430.55 tons

**TOTAL: 9,537 TONS!**

# Help! We're neck deep in trash! What are we going to do?

Recycle, reuse, and, if you have room, compost. That's what we can do. The answer to cutting the amount of garbage that has to be hauled away to landfills that are farther and farther from New York City is obvious: Throw less away. Recycling of bottles, plastic, metal, and paper is the law. Recycling companies turn garbage into things that we can use again. One good way to recycle is not to throw things away if you can use them again yourself. Take plastic bags, for instance. Every year, we toss out enough plastic bags to wrap up the state of Texas. And use cloth towels and napkins instead of paper. Use your lunch bags more than once.

KEEP NEW YORK CLEAN

**JUST SAY NO...TO MENUS**
The average four-family apartment building gets over two pounds of menus, circulars, and handbills every week. That adds up to 200,000 pounds, or 100 tons, per week for the whole city. Believe it or not, this sign will help. You can download one for your door at www.informinc.org/NoMenuSign.pdf.

# SHOCKING RECYCLING FACTS

▶ Seventy-five thousand trees must be cut to make one Sunday edition of the *New York Times*. Seventeen trees are saved if we recycle just one ton of newspaper.

▶ If we recycle all the aluminum trash thrown away in America, we could rebuild the entire U.S. airplane fleet with it every three months.

▶ Once an aluminum can is recycled, it can be part of a new can in six weeks.

▶ If it is not recycled, tin takes 100 years to disappear, aluminum takes 500 years, and glass takes a million years.

▶ Americans throw out enough recyclable paper and plastic cups, forks, and spoons every year to circle Earth at the Equator 300 times.

# Your pal, Skippy, here.

See, I told you. New York City is a wild, wild place to be. And every city and town has wildness woven through it, too, so you can go wild wherever you are. On the next pages, you'll find hot tips for going even further into the wildness of cities to help you and your grown-ups fit in better. All you really do is keep your eyes peeled and your mind open—and don't forget to be nice to squirrels.

# acknowledgments

Creating *Go Wild in New York City* required the love and attention of many, but nothing at all would have happened without Ted Kheel and Nurture New York's Nature. The authors also thank naturalist David Rosane, naturalist David Burg, and geologist Liz Nesbitt; Jake Kheel, Valerie Anderson, Diana Gallic at NNYN; and Amy Zilliax. The designers thank the wonderful photographers especially Cal Vornberger, Maggie Ress, Eliza Gregory, and Diane Shapiro at the Wildlife Conservation Society. Finally, our families were kind enough to put up with us while we were going wild, so thanks to Mary, Laara, Jonas, Milo, Peter, Helena, William, Jeff, Graham, and Lila.

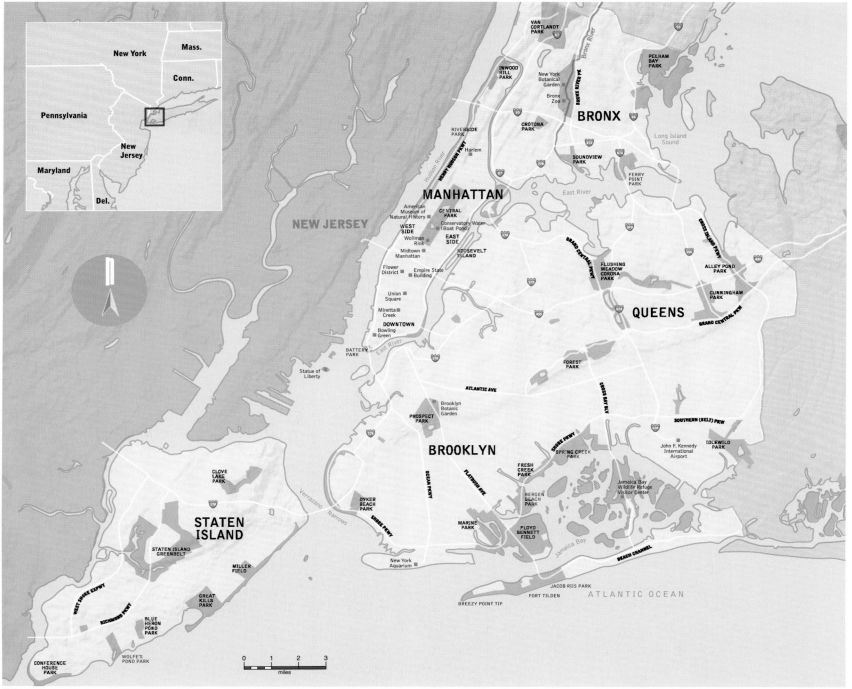

New York

Mass.

Conn.

Pennsylvania

New Jersey

Maryland

Del.

VAN CORTLANDT PARK

PELHAM BAY PARK

INWOOD HILL PARK

New York Botanical Garden

Bronx Zoo

BRONX

CROTONA PARK

Long Island Sound

RIVERSIDE PARK

Harlem

SOUNDVIEW PARK

Henry Hudson Pkwy

Bronx River Pky

MANHATTAN

East River

FERRY POINT PARK

American Museum of Natural History

CENTRAL PARK

Conservatory Water (Boat Pond)

NEW JERSEY

WEST SIDE

Wollman Rink

EAST SIDE

ROOSEVELT ISLAND

CROSS ISLAND PKWY

Hudson River

Midtown Manhattan

FLUSHING MEADOW CORONA PARK

ALLEY POND PARK

Flower District

Empire State Building

GRAND CENTRAL PKWY

CUNNINGHAM PARK

Union Square

QUEENS

Minetta Creek

GRAND CENTRAL PKWY

DOWNTOWN

Bowling Green

BATTERY PARK

East River

FOREST PARK

Statue of Liberty

ATLANTIC AVE

Brooklyn Botanic Garden

CROSS BAY BLVD

PROSPECT PARK

SOUTHERN (BELT) PKW

BROOKLYN

SHORE PKWY

SPRING CREEK PARK

IDLEWILD PARK

John F. Kennedy International Airport

CLOVE LAKE PARK

FRESH CREEK PARK

OCEAN PKWY

FLATBUSH AVE

BERGEN BEACH PARK

Jamaica Bay Wildlife Refuge Visitor Center

STATEN ISLAND

DYKER BEACH PARK

Verrazano Narrows

MARINE PARK

FLOYD BENNETT FIELD

STATEN ISLAND GREENBELT

SHORE PKWY

Jamaica Bay

MILLER FIELD

New York Aquarium

BEACH CHANNEL

WEST SHORE EXPWY

GREAT KILLS PARK

JACOB RIIS PARK

FORT TILDEN

ATLANTIC OCEAN

RICHMOND PKWY

BLUE HERON POND PARK

BREEZY POINT TIP

CONFERENCE HOUSE PARK

WOLFE'S POND PARK

0  1  2  3
miles

# RESOURCES

**Go Wild in New York City is just a taste of all there is to know about New York's nature. If you're craving more info, read on.**

## WILD ABOUT WATER?

**Water Use It Wisely.** There are a number of ways to save the water, and you can learn how at www.wateruseitwisely.com.

**Keep it clean.** To find out about the Clean Water Act, go to www.epa.gov/water.

**Water Wiser,** the water efficiency clearinghouse, is part of the American Water Works Association. To learn how to measure and estimate water wasted due to leaks, go to www.awwa.org/advocacy/learn/conserve/dripcalc.cfm.

**The Goundwater Foundation** is a nonprofit organization dedicated to educating and motivating people to care for and about their groundwater. To learn more, go to www.groundwater.org.

**Hudson River Sloop Clearwater, Inc.** is a non-profit organization created to defend and restore the Hudson River, one of the great and historic rivers of this nation. Reach them at www.clearwater.org.

**The Salt Marsh Alliance,** a not-for-profit organization, was formed in 2002 to supplement city funding for the Salt Marsh Nature Center. To learn how you can become involved, go to www.saltmarshalliance.org.

**NY/NJ Baykeeper's** mission is to protect, preserve, and restore the ecological integrity and productivity of the Hudson-Raritan Estuary—the most urban estuary on the planet. Learn more about them at www.nynjbaykeeper.org.

**Riverkeeper** is an environmental organization devoted to safeguarding the ecological integrity of the Hudson River, its tributaries, and the watershed of New York City by tracking down and stopping polluters. To find out how you can help, visit www.riverkeeper.org.

**Trout in the Classroom** connects kids like you with your watersheds—you may even get to travel upstate to help release trout! Visit www.troutintheclassroom.com to find out more.

## READY TO ROCK?

**The American Museum of Natural History's** site has piles of information about rocks: www.amnh.org/nationalcenter/kids.

**The US Department of Agriculture** lets an animated worm do the talking (about soil) www.nrcs.usda.gov/feature/education/squirm/skworm.html.

**The South Street Seaport** People sift through New York's dirt to find clues about New York's past inhabitants: www.southstreetseaportmuseum.org.

**Earthquakes** can be a scary thing, but you can learn all about them and find out what you need to do in an earthquake at www.fema.gov/kids/ quake.htm.

**Federal Emergency Management Association** teaches you how to be prepared for disasters and prevent disaster damage. You can also learn what causes disasters, play games, read stories, and become a Disaster Action Kid. Visit www.fema.gov/kids to see what's in store.

## HEY, AIRHEAD!

**The U.S. Environmental Protection Agency** wants you to learn more about air. See their site at www.epa.gov/ebtpages/air.html.

**Ozone NY** is New York City's very own online resource for ozone information, www.ozoneny.org.

**Smog City** is an interactive air pollution simulator that shows how your choices, environmental factors, and land use contribute to air pollution. In Smog City you're in control so your visit can be a healthy or unhealthy experience depending on the decisions you make: www.smogcity.com.

**Weather:** To find information about what's going on in the sky anywhere in the country, go to www.weather.com.

**Public Transportation** can help prevent pollution and can be fun. For information on how to use New York's subways, buses, and trains, go to www.mta.nyc.ny.us.

## GOTTA GROW

Plan a trip to the park. See **Central Park's Official Web Site**, for all the information you'll need. Go to www.central parknyc.org to find it.

**New York City Department of Parks & Recreation** can tell you about all of the parks in the New York area, and their site throws in games, and news about events and programs for kids while it's at it. Visit www.nycgovparks.org.

**The Council on the Environment** has a wealth of online information about nurturing nature, including the Grow Truck and the Citizen Street Tree Pruners Course: www.cenyc.org.

**Trees New York** seeks to plant, preserve, protect, and care for New York's trees through education and action. Find their Web site at www.treesny.com.

**The Brooklyn Botanic Garden.** For information on gardening, research, education, and visiting the gardens, go to www.bbg.org.

**New Yorkers for Parks** is a city-wide coalition of civic, greening, recreation, and economic development organizations that serves as an independent advocate for the people of New York and their parks. Find them at www.ny4p.org.

**Riverside Park** on Manhattan's West Side, like many parks, is always looking for more volunteers to help keep it beautiful. Sign up for the next clean-up day, or offer to take a piece of the park under your wing at www.riverside parkfund.org.

**GreenThumb,** the largest community gardening program in the country, is proud to support community gardens in New York City. For more information, go to www.greenthumbnyc.org.

**Green Guerillas'** motto is, "It's your city—dig it." They've been helping people start gardens around town since 1973. Get into the groove by visiting www.greenguerillas.org.

**Green Roof.** Want to create your own green roof? To find out how, go to www.earthpledge.org/GreenRoof.html.

## SPEND QUALITY TIME WITH OTHER CREATURES

Plan a trip to the **Bronx Zoo,** the world's greatest zoo in the world's greatest city, by visiting www.bronxzoo.com.

**New York Aquarium,** where the city meets the sea, can be found online at www.nyaquarium.com.

**The Wildlife Conservation Society** saves wildlife and wild lands through careful science, international conservation, education, and the management of the world's largest system of urban wildlife parks. Visit www.wcs.org for more information.

**The American Zoo and Aquarium Association** (AZA) is a nonprofit organization dedicated to the advancement of zoos and aquariums in the areas of conservation, education, science, and recreation. For more information on their work, or to find a zoo or aquarium anywhere in the United States, go to www.aza.org.

**Monarch Watch,** an educational outreach program, seeks to promote the conservation of Monarch butterflies. To find out what they're all about, visit www.monarchwatch.org.

**Entomological Society of America.** For instructions on how to build an ant farm, visit them at www.entsoc.org/education/elem_mid/ant_habitat.htm.

## HUNGRY FOR FRESHER FOOD?

**Greenmarket** promotes regional agriculture and ensures a continuing supply of fresh, local produce for New Yorkers. Their website can be found at www.cenyc.org. To find out where other green markets are located in New York City, visit www.ny.com/ dining/green.html.

**Earth Pledge's Farm to Table Initiative** aims to educate the public about food and agriculture issues and to guide and support farmers in their transition to sustainable practices. For more information, go to www.farmtotable.org.

## WASTE NOT!

**NYCWasteLe$$** explains how all New Yorkers can save money and reduce waste in their everyday activities. To find out how you can help, go to www.nycwasteless.org.

**The New York City Compost Project** is found at www.nyccompost.org.

**Reduce, Reuse, and Recycle.** Visit the web site of the U.S. Environ-mental Protection Agency at www.epa.gov/epaoswer/non-hw/muncpl/reduce.htm.

**Earth Pledge's Waste=Fuel Initiative.** Want to learn how to turn organic waste into energy? Find out how at www.earthpledge.org/foodwaste.html.

There's an awful lot of wasted food in New York City, but the non-profit food rescue orgzanization **City Harvest** wants to change all that. To find out how, go to www.cityharvest.org.

**No Menus Please!** To get your own "No Menus" sign, go to www.informinc.org/NoMenuSign.pdf

## READY TO GET SERIOUS ABOUT SAVING NATURE?

**The U.S. Environmental Protection Agency** has information about many types of conservation and research. Find them at www.epa.gov.

**Earthpledge** is an organization devoted to identifing and promoting innovative techniques and technologies that restore the balance between human and natural systems. There is lots of great information on this site, so visit www.earthpledge.org.

**The New York City Audubon Society** has the critical task of preserving and protecting grasslands, woodlands, wetlands and wildlife natural habitats throughout New York City. To visit their web site, go to www.nycas.org.

**Alley Pond Environmental Center** is a private, non-profit corporation dedicated to establishing an awareness, understanding and appreciation of the environment and the responsibilities associated with preserving the environment in an urban setting. Their web site is located at www.alleypond.com.

**INFORM** is an independent research organization that examines the effects of business practices on the environment and on human health. They help to educate people on how to reduce pollution and waste, promote sustainable product designs, and convert to cleaner-fueled transportation. See them at www.informinc.org.

## MORE BOOKS TO READ

Margaret Mittlebach and Michael Crewdson. *Wild New York: A Guide to the Wildlife, Wild Places, and Natural Phenomenon of New York City.* Crown Books, 1997.

Murial Winn. *Red-Tails in Love: A Wildlife Drama in Central Park.* Pantheon, 1998.

Jean Gardner and Joel Greenberg. *Urban Wilderness: Nature in New York City.* Earth Environmental Group, 1988.

# credits

**Cover** Central Park: © Cal Vornberger; raccoons: © Diane Shapiro; cicada: © Chris Root/stock.xchng
**Inside Cover** NYC skyline: © Sal Ali, www.mindguerilla.com
**Pages 4 and 5** rock at 181st Street, delivery guy: Eliza N. Gregory; serpentine: Maggie Ress, Jamaica Bay; coyote: © Diane Shapiro; horseshoe crab: © Wildlife Conservation Society; East River: Andrew Shawcross/ShutterPoint; Clearwater: © Chris Bower/Clearwater
**Table of Contents** NYC Sewer Drain: Maggie Ress; lightning: © Greg Geffner; children in garden: Green Guerilla www.greenguerilla.org

WATER
**Page 8** children in park: Eliza N. Gregory
**Page 9** Broadway, Minetta Street, Chambers Street, Third Ave, Brooklyn: Maggie Ress; Croton Reservoir: © NYC Dept. of Environmental Protection; bowling green: Jeffrey Murphy; Criminal Courts building: consultwebs.com; Harlem River: © ThinkStock/Getty Images
**Page 11** City Water Tunnel: © NYC Dept. of Environmental Protection
**Page 13** glass of water: AGE FotoStock; cement factory: Gary Donnelly/ShutterPoint
**Page 15, cover** NYC manhole cover: Maggie Ress
**Page 16** East River: Andrew Shawcross/ShutterPoint; Bronx River: ©Tamara W. Hill, www.tamarahillphotography.com; Jamaica Bay: © Diane Shapiro; Clearwater: © Chris Bower/Clearwater

ROCKS
**Page 18** rock wall footer, serpentine: Maggie Ress; hartland rocks: Eliza N. Gregory
**Page 20** aerial of Coney Island: © Joseph R. Melanson of www.skypic.com; rock at 181st Street: Eliza N. Gregory
**Page 21** rock, Flatbush Ave: Eliza N. Gregory; Park Slope: © ipvStudio.com
**Page 22** blass bldg detail: Eliza N. Gregory
**Page 23** boulder: Eliza N. Gregory
**Page 25** Subway tunnel: Eliza N. Gregory
**Page 26** rocks: Maggie Ress
**Page 27** worm: © E. Degginger/Color-Pic, Inc.; worm background: Mayang

WEATHER
**Page 29** NYC skyline clear: © Robert Blackman/Shutterpoint
**Page 30** NYC bus: Eliza N. Gregory
**Page 33** NYC skyline: © Sal Ali www.mindguerilla.com

**Page 34** NYC in the snow: Comstock/Getty; hurricane: NOAA; NYC lightning: © Greg Geffner; clouds: Eliza N. Gregory; Verranzano in fog: © Steve Wandy/Shutterpoint
**Page 35** roof garden: © Heather Sommerfield/ Earth Pledge; Highline trail: © Josh Rogers /The Villager

PLANTS
**Page 36** pansies: Maggie Ress
**Page 40** Van Cortland Park: Eliza N. Gregory; Pelham Bay Park, Greenbelt Staten Island: Bianca Colasuonno/Wild Metro
**Page 41** NY Botanical garden sign, Weird bush: Eliza N. Gregory; vanilla orchid: John M. Coffman
**Page 43** daffodils, cherry blossoms, dandelion, wild-flowers: Maggie Ress; Pink Lady Slippers: © Eric Hunt; rose garden: Eliza N. Gregory
**Page 44** community garden volunteers (bottom image), mural painting: Green Guerilla; rhubarb: Eliza N. Gregory; radishes, community garden sign, green beans: Maggie Ress
**Page 45** garden shop, window box, onions: Eliza N. Gregory; radishes, tomatoes: Maggie Ress

BUGS
**Page 47** dragonfly: stock.xchng
**Page 48** large cockroach: Joao Estevao A. de Frietas/stock.xchng
**Page 49** cockroach: © E. Derringer/Color-Pic, Inc.
**Page 50** praying mantis: © Natasha Vincent/stock.xchng; june bug: © Michal Napartowicz/stock.xchng; dung beetle: J. Delaney/© Wildlife Conservation Society; damsel fly: © Martin Kessel/stock.xchng; window skimmer, Eastern Swallowtail: © Cal Vornberger; firefly: © E. Derringer/Color-Pic, Inc.
**Page 51** beekeeper David Graves: © Cal Vornberger
**Page 52** spider: © Margus Kyatta/stock.xchng
**Page 53** wasp, bee with pollen, wasp on flower: © Cal Vornberger; ladybug: © Brunakta/stock.xchng; ants on fruit: © Diane Shapiro; dermestid beetle: courtesy Maxible& Mandible
**Page 54** cicada: © Chris Root/stock.xchng; gypsy moth: © Diane Shapiro
**Page 55** monarch caterpillar, butterfly: © Cal Vornberger

ANIMALS
**Page 56** dog walker: © Robert Hausmann; cat, guinea pig: © Diane Shapiro
**Page 57** Iguana: C. Rogus © Wildlife Conservation Society; chinchilla on bookcase: © E. Derringer/Color-Pic, Inc.

**Page 58 and 59** coyote, chipmunk, raccoon pups, Eastern cottontail: © Diane Shapiro; opposum, skunks: © Betty Groskin; muskrat: D. DeMellow © Wildlife Conservation Society
**Page 61** NYPD on horses: Maggie Ress; carousel in Central Park: Eliza N. Gregory
**Page 62** Eastern Common garter snake: © Wildlife Conservation Society; clam: © Diane Shapiro; horse-shoe crab: © Wildlife Conservation Society; snapping turtle: © E. Degginger/Color-Pic, Inc.
**Page 63** brook trout: © Diane Shapiro; bullfrog: C. Rogus/ © Wildlife Conservation Society; fisherman at 130th street: Eliza N. Gregory
**Page 64** Jamaica Bay: © Diane Shapiro; perrigrine falcon: © Betty Groskin
**Page 65** great blue heron: © Wildlife Conservation Society; hooded merganser: B. Meng © Wildlife Conservation Society; screech owl, house finch; black-capped chickadee: M. DaRocha/ © Wildlife Conservation Society; great egret, redtail hawk: B. Levenson © Wildlife Conservation Society; pigeons: Eliza N. Gregory

FOOD
**Page 66** grocery store: Maggie Ress
**Page 67** chicken on grill: © Conrad Czarnecki/stock.xchng; coffee cart, Chinese restaurant, outdoor café: Eliza N. Gregory; outdoor Chinese market: Maggie Ress
**Page 68 and 69** delivery guy, delivery truck, tomato plants, Union Square Market, strawberries for sale: Eliza N. Gregory
**Page 67** garbage can and door stoop: Maggie Ress

All other photography provided by Katherine Dillon and Kate Thompson of DillonThompson LLC.

# index

**Bold type** indicates illustrations.

**A**

Air conditioning 33, **33**

Air pollution 28, 30, 35, 61, 69

Alligators **14**;

   living in sewers 14;

   as pets 57

Animals, wild 58, **58–59**

Ants 51, 52, **53**;

ant farm **51**

Aquariums 63

Atmosphere 28-33, 35

Avocado seed experiment 38, **38**

**B**

Bedrock **12**, 18–19, **19**, 25

Bees and wasps 51, **51**, 52, 53, **53**

Bird watching 64, 65

Birds 52, 58, 64–65, **64–65**

Breathing 29, 30, 33, 36

Bricks 22, **22**

Butterflies and moths **50**, 52, **54**, 55, **55**

**C**

Cats 56, **56**

Centipedes 52, **52**

Chocolate-covered insects 51

Cicadas 54, **54**

Climate 32, 33

Clouds 8, 10, **30–31**, 31

Cockroaches 47–49, **48–49**, 52

Corpse flowers 42

Creeks and streams 9, 10, 16, 63

**D**

Daffodil Project 42

Dermestid beetles 53, **53**

Dirt 26, **26**, 27, 45

Dogs **30**, 36, 56, **56**

**E**

Earthquakes 25

Exotic pets 57, **57**

**F**

Farms 28, 44, 69

Fault lines 25, **25**

Fish **62**, 63;

as pets 58, 63

Fishing 63, **63**; bait 27

Flies 52, 54

Flowers 35, **36**, 42–43, **42–43**, 44, **45**

Fruits and vegetables 35, 44, **45**, **66–69**, 68–69

**G**

Garbage 61, 64, 66, 70–71, **70–71**

Gardens and gardening 44–45, **44–45**;

   botanical gardens 41;

   compost 27, 45, 71;

   "green roofs" 35, **35**

Giant tree 38, **38**

Green markets 66, 69, **69**

**H**

Horses 61, **61**

Horseshoe crabs 62, **62**

Humidity 31

Humus 26, **26**, 27

Hydrologic cycle 10, **10**

**I**

Ice age 20–21

**L**

Landfills 70, 71

**M**

Metamorphosis 55, **55**

Monarch butterflies 55, **55**

**P**

Parks **40**, 40–41, 58, 61, 62

Pets 56–57, **56–57**

Photosynthesis 37, **37**

Pigeons 64, **65**, 68

Plates, tectonic 18, **18**, 19, 25

Pollen and pollination 43, 52, 53

Ponds 63;

   pond scum **36**

**R**

Rats 58, 60, **60**

Recycling 71

Restaurants 66, **67**, 68, 69

Rivers 8, 10, 15, 16, **16**, 63

Rock climbing 23, **23**

Rock collecting 24, **24**

**S**

Salt marshes 16, **16**

Sewage plants **14–15**, 15

Sinks and toilets 8, 12, 14, **14**, 15, 17

Snakes 56, 57, 62, **62**

Snapping turtles 62, **62**

Spiders 47, 52, **52**, 62

Squirrel **4**, 58, 61, 68, **72**

**T**

Tiger, pet 57

Tracks, animal **58**

Trees 36, **36**, 38–39, **38–39**;

   champion tree 38, **38**;

   insect damage 39, 54;

   saving 71

Trout-growing program 63

Tunnels, water 8, 10–11, **10–11**, 12

**W**

Water cycle 10, **10**, 17

Water pollution 15, 16, 33, 63

Weather 32–34;

   extremes 34;

   role of cities 33;

   weather maps **32**

Weeds 36, **36**, 42

Wild preserves 41

Wildlife 58, **58–59**

Worms 27, **27**

**Z**

Zoos 57